The Middle of Ordinary

Monica Rae

I was thirteen when I wanted to be thirty…

The barred windows and cold chairs did nothing to ease my apprehension—neither did the fear buried under my mother's forced smile. The unheard-of diagnosis changed the landscape of my adolescence. Its loneliness would chase me out of childhood. The grip of its symptoms and rejection would drive me into patient advocacy and a quest for healing.

The sound of your cry would release me and redefine my concept of love. Your presence would challenge my roots and show me what I was capable of.

And so, it's for you, my child, that I write this book…

Table of Contents

Prologue

Chapter 1 Pain's Purpose   page   9

Chapter 2 The Point is the Serve   page   29

Chapter 3 Cul-de-sac Roots   page   47

Chapter 4 After Innocence   page   61

Chapter 5 Is Faith Enough?   page   75

Chapter 6 In the Company of Men and Dogs   page   87

Chapter 7 Prairie Sermons   page 109

Chapter 8 The Extraordinary Lessons   page 127

The Middle of Ordinary: Lesson Guide   page 149
    Questions to guide and reflect on your reading

Prologue

*I hadn't met you, but I knew you. As though from a dream you
appeared, dark eyed and determined...*

The stench of gasoline made me nauseous like never before. I was
sore, tired and visited the bathroom every 30 minutes. It took three
at-home tests and one doctor's visit to confirm what I already knew.
Fear and excitement raged through me as the nurse uttered three words
that changed my life forever. "You are pregnant!"

Eight months later you appeared—with my eyes, hair, and lips. I
was not surprised. Your eager spirit brought you three weeks early,
still scoring a perfect score on your APGAR test. Born with an
eagerness to explore the world on your cautious terms, you yet
believed around every bend was a reason to smile.

What would catch me by surprise and teach me to move beyond
my melancholy tendencies, the diseases that plagued me and the
traditional roots that I came from was your unrelenting joy. That joy
would open the gates of my pierced spirit. You would teach me to
dream without fear, love without reservations and hope without doubt.
And we would walk this road together as mother and daughter and
teacher and student.

The list is long, the questions I asked my parents as I sought clarity
and purpose trying to equip my young mind with answers necessary
to navigate adulthood. My mother would oblige with age-appropriate
answers, all the while I'm sure, wishing the endless game of twenty

questions would cease.

Like me, you are thoughtful and curious—and have begun to ask questions, some of which I'd rather not answer! But I want you to know how you came to be. And to do that you must understand my life's journey.

These letters are a reflection on that journey—the lessons of pain and disappointment, the blessing and awe. And how becoming your mother brought me the greatest joy I will ever know.

Chapter 1 – Pain's Purpose

"The world breaks everyone, and afterwards many are strong in the broken places." Ernest Hemingway

My dearest,

I was yearning for darkness, for a quiet hole I could crawl into. My body was in throbbing pain like someone had thrown me in a dryer on 'high tumble.' Beating relentlessly against the walls I had to push through; I had to pretend that I had hidden the unwelcome visitor of pain in the closet. I had to do this because you were two and four and ten and I never wanted you to know the truth behind our so-called 'days at home.'

There is a point of no return when you are diagnosed with a chronic illness—a point of surrender, but not of defeat.

When I was thirteen years old, I didn't know what the word 'diagnosis' meant, but apparently, that's what my mom and I were searching for with each doctor's appointment. It had been months since a severe case of pneumonia had left me extremely pale, severely weakened and fatigued. Being an adolescent is difficult enough—hormones shooting in every direction like an uncontrollable firework show, my classmates' and peers' opinions far more influential than the 40-something parental figures in my home. Add to that a diagnosis of a mystery illness and I felt like "outsider" had been written on my forehead, creating an invisible barricade around me. Only my mother would dare enter.

The doctor walked into the room with quiet yet confident grace, his Middle Eastern accent riveted our attention. A middle-aged child neurologist in the California valley, he had experience treating children of all ages experiencing seizures, neurological disorders and presenting the nightmare diagnoses that parents dread. It was his calmness as he gave the truth to my mom and me that made us believe there was hope—not in the form of relief, but in a name.

Over a year of testing, poking, prodding, suffering glares from doctors, the ignorance of family and friends and, finally, we had it. There was a time when I thought I'd never get an answer. At one point I was in tears as our family doctor attempted to explain to my mother and me in the most diplomatic way possible that it was *all in my head*. But all those fears subsided the day my mom and I were greeted by Dr. Asaikar.

We had to drive miles into the heart of the city to find his office. I could tell that we were no longer in our suburbia when my mom began to glance with concern at every person who walked by. I followed my mother's lead and made sure I didn't leave anything in the car that I didn't want to be stolen. We took the elevator and walked the dark hallway to the office. I opened the door, and a wave of apprehension encased me. Was this going to be a waste of time? I saw other children around me, younger and wheelchair bound, some unable to speak, others pounding on the table back in the corner—a parent's attempt at confining the unpredictable youngster. A little girl still in a stroller, unable to talk, her head wrapped in bandages—her smile was both sweet and sad. Did she know her enemy, pain, already? Was her mind trapped somewhere not even her mother could get to?

I found no comfort in my surroundings, no solace in these young faces. It would be years before I could see myself in them—not the same diagnosis or even the same prognosis, but a shared understanding of the isolating pain that comes with uncertainty.

We had a name for the darkness that had crept into my life—the diagnosis that would impact my adolescent reality and, ultimately, my whole life. Chronic Fatigue Immune Dysfunction Syndrome (CFIDS) they named it. Awful name! The word 'fatigue' left many people to conclude that as a patient you had given up, that all that was necessary for relief was mental determination, a strong cup of coffee or a five-hour energy drink.

The average, healthy person has no awareness of this fatigue. It's the fatigue you feel on the worst day of having the flu, when lifting your spoon to enjoy your soup creates a pain message that radiates through your whole body. It's rising from the bed after twelve hours of unrefreshed sleep and placing your feet on the floor creating a release of neurotransmitters that mixed up the message—this isn't supposed to be painful! But it doesn't just take up residence in your arms and legs; it's all-consuming in its efforts to haunt you. A beautiful sunny day becomes your worst enemy as the brightness sends you running for cover or, at the very least, dark glasses and a large hat. Sounds of laughter and screams of delight are hammers on your ears, echoing like a never-ending trombone in an unwelcome parade.

I had been given a name for the symptoms that wouldn't subside, but, in reality, I knew nothing because over 30 years ago not much was known about an illness that affects over one million people in the USA alone. At that time there was minimal testing, a broad spectrum of symptoms and a handful of physicians who believed they could treat these unrelenting and unpredictable flare-ups and seemingly defeated patients.

Dr. Asaikar's even-tempered demeanor and confident grasp of my symptoms filled me with hope. Doubt was replaced with a diagnosis. He recommended one of the only books written at that time by a doctor who had become a fierce advocate for patients and families, Dr. David Bell. My mother made a quick escape to the nearest bookstore to purchase a copy that sits on my bookshelf, highlighted and dogeared to this day.

At 13 years old, I began my fierce plunge into research and the minimal information I found was discouraging. Decades ago, the most popular correlation was to mononucleosis, 'aka' the *kissing disease*, because the flu-like symptoms hinted at a viral agent. This false theory was quickly put to rest when tests revealed most CFIDS patients had never been infected with mono. Of course, such rumors did nothing to ease the panicky patients and confused medical community who sought answers.

Further research proved its isolation—CFIDS was, in fact, a multifaceted disease—with unexplainable manifestations through various systems within the body, with no singular cause. But the disease would remain clouded with uncertainty, and it would be decades before any strides in research brought explanations.

Mainstream artists, authors and athletes like Laura Hillenbrand, Cher, Stevie Nicks, and Olympic star Michelle Akers would begin to shed light on the plight that so many patients face each day.

CFIDS appears in patients of all ages, although a significant percentage of them are older adult women. Like many diseases, the range of severity varies from patient to patient—making it difficult for physicians to give a clear prognosis. Some patients have manageable flare-ups of symptoms that subside within months or years, often brought on by other acute illnesses, surgeries or major life stressors— more unfortunate patients would come to understand why the word 'chronic' was attached to its name.

The 'fatigue' that the disease is named for only highlights one of the multitude of symptoms that encompass this disease. The list is long: night sweats, unrefreshing sleep, stomach and digestive abnormalities, random fevers, paleness, aching or burning pain throughout the body, sensitivity to light and sound, food sensitivities, memory and cognitive dysfunction, and weakened immune system function among others. Depression and anxiety often accompany patients after months of symptoms leave them feeling unable to function as they once did. And over time many patients including myself would succumb to other diagnoses as the immune system became weakened. In the almost 30 years since my original diagnosis, I have developed Fibromyalgia (FMS), Intercystical Cystitis (IC), peripheral neuropathy, breast tumors, skin abnormalities, a swollen spleen, and *multiple* infections of pneumonia and Shingles.

The symptoms came and went without warning like riding a roller coaster with your eyes closed. I began to expect the symptoms as though they had a power all of themselves. Relief was a precious commodity, a needle in a haystack, a four-leaf clover waiting to be found. It would be years before I realized I couldn't be fooled by hours or days of relief, modalities that eased the symptoms or even sunny days that felt like warm blankets of wonder instead of hell on earth—I knew what peril was awaiting me upon my return to the corridor of pain.

Many patients suffer years before they find consistent relief, often battling flare-ups of symptoms. In the worst cases, patients are left bedridden. I have seen the lives of some ripped apart by the aggressiveness of symptoms, leaving them a tattered version of who they once were.

A middle-aged woman and fellow patient approached me when I was in my early 20's. She said she felt such sympathy for me—that someone my age had to deal with such a debilitating disease. I looked at her and smiled. I said quietly, "I've never known anything different, and in that way, it's a blessing." I came to know many patients during my years of advocacy. Most were middle-aged or older and, in my opinion, theirs was the greater struggle. They and their families were haunted by memories of careers and social lives that were unscarred by CFIDS. I had been spared this contrast, and in that way, I was blessed by my early diagnosis. But when I was 13 years old, I was still in the clutches of adolescent euphoria, uncertain of how the 'chronic' part of my new visitor of pain was going to dictate my future.

"Where were you?" my classmates asked—a three-yard distance from me, as though I had returned to school armed to infect them! Preteens were walking through the halls of their territory saturated in the stench of rumors, gripping their chosen social group carefully. Friends that once greeted me with hugs and the latest 'who likes who' were now afraid of my pale complexion in their classroom.

Teachers were just as confused about my absence but not because of the social implications or even out of fear of catching this unheard-of disease. I had never fallen behind in my assignments, always maintaining a high GPA, eager to impress them with my love of learning and I would return with the same attitude as I left with. But for some teachers, this was 'unacceptable' and my grades needed to reflect a sort of punishment for my absence. Teachers in high school and occasional professors in college would dock my grades to communicate their displeasure and confusion regarding my absences that spanned weeks and sometimes months.

I remember within weeks of my return to school, being in the courtyard where the excitable and hormone-driven masses gathered to fill up on sugar and hot lunch. In the California valley where I grew up, school campuses faced outside. Lockers, lunch areas, and hallways were all outdoors as the temperatures kept winters mild and therefore no need for a complete enclosure. I was navigating the social groups—those made popular by their looks or their parents' money, jocks, druggies, nerds and the religious middle class—when a boy who I knew only as an acquaintance had a genius idea. He threw a full soda across the courtyard and it smashed itself instantly against my head, exploding over my head, clothes and the ground around me.

Blood began to rush down the side of my face as the boy appeared at my side. He was cautious though, concerned about the validity of the recent rumors—I was the pale classmate who he'd seen return to the hallways of our shared province. Maybe he realized I wasn't a vampire out for his blood or a still-infected alien ready to unleash my venom upon him—either way; he seemed to decide rather quickly I was 'cool' enough to accompany to the nurse's office. Very apologetic in the days to come, he 'checked in' with me during each hallway run in, making sure my ten stitches were healing and that I had forgiven him for his foolish antics. Weeks passed and our 'hallway doctor visits' began to fade into brief glances and appeasing smiles. I was certain I had added more confusion to my already tainted junior high reputation.

A few months later he approached me, a yearbook in hand, beaming with cautious excitement as he stopped me in the hallway. "I got enough votes for you to be in the hall of fame," he declared pridefully. I glanced at the page he had propped open—I was surprised to find underneath the pale, sickly picture of myself the caption "Voted Shyest in Our Class." At first, I was slightly embarrassed, for I hadn't been chosen as the prettiest or most likely to succeed, but this vote of confidence would suffice. I had been acknowledged by my peers and that would travel through the escalades of my high school years – that pure satisfaction was a stark contrast to the last year I had experienced.

The first year after diagnosis was characterized in one word, "outsider," but my high school would at least *begin* with the opposite tune. I had found solace from the bruising and awkwardness of CFIDS in a local church youth group. My symptoms would define my abilities, but they didn't shake my desire for the typical teenage experience I longed to engage in.

For close to 4 years, I threw myself into the social and religious expectations of the Baptist church I began attending with a childhood friend, Katie, and her family. Katie and I met in kindergarten and lived over a mile from each other. We regularly met for girl time adventures—swimming, building forts, listening to music and playing with our newest Barbies. But my favorite moments would be spent walking with her to the tiny frozen yogurt shop they opened a mile east of our neighborhood. When I began to get sick, many friends and subsequently their parents stayed away for fear of the unknown, yet Katie and her family remained steadfast in their affection.

I navigated the pitfalls of my teenage years with my new roommate of pain becoming quite familiar. But I began to sense a struggle—the daily demands of my illnesses leaving me unable to completely connect with the expectations of family, peers and those in the religious circle I had entered. The tiredness and pain would be consistent in its unpredictability, but I would find modalities such as physical therapy, medicine and sleep routines to counter the attacks. So, in my attempt to learn to live with CFIDS, I found it startling to encounter a different kind of pain. And while my illnesses would teach me responsibility before most pre-teens could define the word, I would get a glimpse of the final nudge out of my youth—the isolating rejection of those from whom I least expected it.

Sympathy was awkward as family members, who knew nothing beyond the numerous doctor appointments years prior, were left unsure of how to act or what to say. My mother, staying true to form, was persistent and unwavering in her support.

The image of my mom during my childhood and adolescence was one of staunch attention. I was spoiled by her desire to fix my pain in any way she could. But in turn, I depended on her completely even as I began to feel the natural tendencies for independence that encompassed my adolescence. I felt heard and accepted in the presence of my mother. She couldn't take away the realities of my disease or the rejection of those around me but would listen, never telling me to stop crying and always trying to make the day better with a purchase from a nearby store or mall.

Many days she would return home from work carrying bags of groceries, trinkets to add to the shelves and drawers of my room, clothes or shoes I didn't have the energy to go try on, movies she thought I would enjoy or projects she thought I could work on. As a mother, I understand her desire to 'do' amid her child's suffering—to feel like you are helping in any way seems more fruitful than sitting idle. I applaud her efforts and understand the worry and isolation that overcame her, but at the time all I saw was my own.

My extended family had such a limited scope of information regarding my illnesses, whether they chose to stay ignorant of the realities of my diseases out of laziness or pride I'm not sure. But years later, I would come to find out there was an influx of comments relayed to my mother from relatives who just didn't understand but were quick to judge my reality and my mom's supportive response to it. How isolating that must have been for her.

I think for years my father and sister just didn't know what to say. They never rejected my presence or presumed to know how to fix my ailment, but I could feel their sense of frustration at my inabilities. My father, the salesman with 10-hour work days, and my sister, about to turn 16 years old when I was reaching a diagnosis, were understandably involved in the demands of their obligations and ages. They had seen me exhausted after minimal exertion, fevers after school, sleeping for 10 hours straight and in pain after days of a normal routine but, as with most things that need explaining, it's the unseen and unpredictable that we are haunted by most.

These painful episodes were sprinkled with my attempts at normalcy—my devotion to academia and church and my desire for an ordinary social experience. I would go on a date on Friday night and sleep till noon on a Saturday morning. I would read books by the fireplace when my sister was leaving for work. After socializing with friends, I was too exhausted to be much assistance to my mother. I wanted to fit in with the other girls my age, be liked by a hormone-driven boy and be thought of as 'cool' in the eyes of my all-knowing older sister. I longed to be normal and yet was tired of trying to fit in. And so, with no physical evidence that remained progressive, I continued to be a teenage anomaly.

Years later, in an attempt to understand the impact my illness had on those around me, I turned my college psychology thesis into an in-depth study of the effect of chronic diseases on siblings.

My first glance at research suggested a presence of isolation in siblings of the chronically ill, causing them to either fight for their parents' affection or be driven to a lifestyle of independent accomplishment. My sister would be the latter. I was faced with the reality that my disease had affected the three people I lived with – each in different ways. As a young adult, I wasn't sure if I should apologize, leave quietly or explain myself further. So, I sent the research paper to my parents and sister, along with subsequent findings, articles, and books in the years that followed, hoping to clarify my reality, implore their understanding and heal the wound that seemed to be left by the presence of my illnesses.

"I met with experiences that bruised my spirit - but they never harmed my ideal world. That was always mine to retreat into at will....I found that it was useless to look for kindred souls in the multitude; one might stumble on such here and there, but as a rule, it seemed to me that the majority of people lived for the things of time and sense alone and could not understand my other life. So I piped and danced to other people's piping - and held fast to my own soul as best I could." — L.M. Montgomery

Unlike most kids, I was neither eager nor excited about learning to drive. So, I waited till I was past 17 years old before I got my license. Driving for most teens means freedom, for me, it meant energy loss and pain. To this day, driving is the least popular demand on my time.

I will drive to get to work, the weekly grocery run, get you to all your activities each week, or because I want you to experience the world, but I'd just rather not.

So, at the end of my junior year in high school, with much reluctance, I acquired my license, added to that a job at a local book store and took a life-altering trip during the summer to visit a friend who had moved to Sioux Falls, South Dakota to attend seminary.

Within five months, my pain had flared to incorrigible levels, leaving me home-tutored, without a job and without much use for the gray Mercury Topaz that sat in my parents' driveway. Doctors would discover that my immune system had been hijacked by an infection it couldn't adequately fight and my white blood and killer T cell counts were hovering dangerously low. And if that wasn't enough, now I was dealing with a new diagnosis. A locally-recommended rheumatologist would shake his head in certain disbelief as he relayed to my neurologist that I had acquired a disease common to the middle-aged and elderly—Fibromyalgia Syndrome (FMS). Almost unfazed by the common trips to the doctors whose care I was under, I was even less surprised by the new set of symptoms I was going to have to learn to manage, for this disease came with a mishmash of recommendations and no cure.

Fibromyalgia Syndrome (FMS), Chronic Fatigue Immune Dysfunction Syndrome (CFIDS) and other similar conditions form a family of overlapping syndromes. In fact, researcher Muhammad Yunus, M.D., of the University of Illinois College of Medicine, claims that up to 75% of patients have both. FMS and CFIDS are part of a larger gamut of conditions which could be referred to as a dysregulation of bio-physiological systems—including the body's immune, chemical, hormonal and neurological centers. Unlike CFIDS—which is characterized more by unrelenting fatigue, FMS is diagnosed through identifying trigger points over the entire body. In these places, patients feel a variety of pain experiences ranging from tender and inflamed to bruised, aching or throbbing. While progress has been made in areas of international research and advocacy since my diagnosis over 20 years ago, many patients still struggle to find a local physician who dares to enter the unforgiving nature of these illnesses.

I spent the majority of my senior year of high school at home. A tutor began to come to the house with my school assignments and I checked in with my teachers every couple weeks regarding tests and presentations. I would rather read a novel than sneak out to a party, so the credits required to graduate were quickly accumulated six months before my senior year's graduation ceremony. With the arrival of spring came a phone call from a long-time friend, Jeremy, who was never fazed by the presence of the illness. He insisted I go to the Senior Prom. Not with him, of course, as he already had a date, but just as a tag along so I wouldn't miss out on the experience. I knew I'd be tired by 8 pm and wouldn't enjoy the feeling of being without a date, so I reluctantly declined.

I would attend a few such social affairs in college, thinking I had somehow missed out. But looking back, I wasn't overcome with a desire to be shoulder to shoulder with the awkwardness of 'almost' men and women dressed in tight-fitting clothes, bragging about the drinks they snuck in their pockets or money they paid for a limousine to drive their date to the chaperoned event. It was more the idea that the pain in my body seemed to dictate what I could and couldn't do that left me discouraged. The feeling of normalcy that had existed for a couple of years in high school was quickly descending into a shy shame that I didn't know how to put into words.

The sound of peers would begin to dissipate in fear of the unknown. Girlfriends would be busy with mall runs and part-time jobs, while boys would call but never stay around long as they were in hot pursuit of girls that enjoyed more than a good book. So, I began to take up long-distance fellowships with friends and cousins I had met on my recent trip to the Midwest. Those relationships were a sustaining escape from my local reality. The letters, emails and phone calls were exchanged on my 'good days,' making it easier to hide the reality of my disease.

How does a daughter chrysalis into a new skin of womanhood when it is painful to leave the house? There is a great shame in chronic pain—the feeling of inadequacy haunts me to this day. But the self-conscious nature of a teenager, packed tightly with hormones, driven mostly by emotion, left me almost certain that the only way to escape the pain, the only way to find purpose, would be to leave my California roots. But where would a disease-stricken, bookworm who despised driving go? I would take up solace in the prairie, the southeast corner pocket of the state and largest city in South Dakota—Sioux Falls.

The greatest teachers I've known have been the illnesses that have plagued me.

I began to navigate my Midwestern home as an adult—determined to find purpose in my pain. I danced the waltz of sickness again in my 20s and 30s when doctors found a disease in the lining of my stomach, multiple breast tumors, peripheral neuropathy and an infection in my spleen. Years of multiple cases of pneumonia left my immune system in a constant heightened state. In an unfazed daze, I would relay the newest diagnosis to my worry-stricken mother 2,000 miles away. She never wavered in her attention to detail and hung to the words of my physicians—their prognosis became her road map to the diseases I fought so far away from her.

Reading became my escape into the world I couldn't touch or travel to but could experience in my mind. Days used for functioning (college, work, chores, church or travel) were followed by a rest day when lights were dimmed, makeup was off, and stacks of books were at my bedside. And then I became a mother, and you grew taller and wiser, and I couldn't hide behind my pages any longer. Now my inabilities were exposed. I had traded my stack of books and hours of uninterrupted rest for fear—what could I offer you in my pain?

In this world of bigger is better, 1st place is the only place and instant gratification I would be challenged by the presence of what I couldn't do. I was like the waxing and waning of a rope being pulled in two different directions—each side of arms taking turns gaining on the other—so close to leaving one side slamming to the ground.

Just as soon as I began to experience the satisfaction of a workday finished, a class taught or chores completed, I would be overcome with the return of pain, like a spit in my face. My arms ached, my eyes unable to carry the weight of contact with another person, my legs weak from moving to the bathroom, my brain now a foreign entity unable to remember a recipe I memorized years before or the address of the friend you had been to just a week before. My sunglasses are snug on the top of my head most days when I leave the house. The sunglasses a superhero's cape, a convenient covering for my pain— sparkles on the side allowing me to smile in my embarrassment. You became a member of the chosen few who would ever see me on my days of vulnerability. I trusted that you'd keep my weakness a secret, but I hated that my pain had become a member of our family.

I thought I had made peace with its presence in the years I lived on my own. As you grew though, I had to take my inabilities out of hiding. I kept a meticulous calendar, sprinkled with your activities, playtimes with friends and school reminders. I was so determined to give you the best of myself, so clear in my purpose as your mother and homeschool teacher. And yet as you grew you saw the subtle differences between my routine and other parents. I would retreat to my bedroom many nights after tucking you in and I would sleep two hours longer than you on rest days. You gathered your second wind when I was ready for a nap, and you had little experience with road trips because driving was my greatest energy rival. While other mothers could work fulltime jobs or juggle a family of many children,

I had "days of rest" and "staying at home" sprinkled tirelessly in between your school, dance, swim and art lessons.

"When life is rosy, we may slide by with knowing about Jesus, with imitating him and quoting him and speaking of him. But only in suffering will we know Jesus." Joni Eareckson Tata

Through the gospels, I am reminded of how committed Jesus was to what his purpose was even amidst the isolation, despair, and disappointment that he knew he would encounter. Throughout my journey of sickness, I have questioned my life's worth. I've shaken my fist and demanded a response to my seemingly insignificant life. And, even more than relief, I've desired peace and joy—the two elements of contentment of which my constant pain robs me. And so, it is both ironic and wonderous that the unpredictable and unrelenting ailments would show me a way out of my pain.

For years I was prayed for and prayed over. Even as I attended a Christian liberal arts college, classmates informed me that my prayers would release me from the physical abuse the illnesses had brought me. Apparently, my problem wasn't pain; I had a lack of faith that was causing my illnesses! I was appalled by their responses. I developed a thick skin to such responses as I would be on the receiving end of well-intentioned friends, family members, strangers, and colleagues throughout my life who felt compelled to inform me of the latest book, remedy, diet, medicine or devotional that would fix me. It would be years before I learned that the "Judas sector" of people exists in the lives of most people and I was no different.

My epiphany came in full surrender, not to the demands of my illnesses or defeat by those who rejected me, but in serving the suffering people that surrounded me. Their illnesses came in the form of FMS and CFIDS, but also in chronic, unrelenting migraines, seizures, cancer, depression, heartache, job loss, poverty, divorce, emotional abuse. I was the image of every man and woman facing loss and the demands and confusion that surrounded them.

And it was then, somewhere in the midst of serving patients in my 20s and motherhood in my 30s, that I wanted to go back to the children sitting in the waiting room when I met the neurologist who gave me my life-changing diagnosis. I wanted to hug them and look them in the eyes and tell them that while I had a different disease, I understood their loneliness. And while I couldn't take their pain away, I knew a love beyond our understanding that would give purpose to the pain.

The purpose for my life couldn't be found in a cure – it had to be found in a *creator*, who had given me life and an opportunity to find a peace that was more necessary than my relief.

The greatest teacher you will know will be the journey just past your comfort, the place where fear and torment tease your spirit, and you wonder if you'll ever find relief. It's there that you will begin to understand what you are capable of. It will scare you, my child, and make you wonder where God is, and when you realize you are being carried; it will finally become clear how strong you are.

Chapter 2 – The Point is To Serve

"I do not know what your destiny will be, but of one thing I am certain—the only ones among you who will be truly happy are those who have sought and found how to serve."

Dr. Albert Schweitzer

My child,

Manila, the capital of the Philippines, was scattered with rhythmic chaos—horns beeping, children half-naked, yelling in the streets, tall buildings casting shadows on the traffic below, taxi cabs crowded with locals and the occasional out-of-place businessman in a hurry to get to his high-rise hotel. I was gazing out the window of my room on the 20th floor, afraid of heights yet captivated by the landscape so different from my home. This country is a canvas covered with natural and untouched beauty—mountains and beaches that define most people's perception of paradise. And yet, as I looked out the window, I was struck not by the beauty of its natural landscape but by the beauty of its people. After almost a month staying with a friend who was there on business, I had come to know the people—their hospitality, so generous in the middle of their poverty and suffering. And their response to adversity would be my muse as I continued in advocating and serving patients suffering from chronic illnesses.

There was a knock at the door; time for my late morning exchange with the young man, age 17 or 18, whose name I never learned how to pronounce correctly. But during my month's stay in Manila, he would make sure I had fresh towels and linens and anything else I needed. He shared with me that his mother and father had died and that he had two young sisters and a brother to care for in the ghetto. I had come to learn enough about the economic structure of Manila and much of the Philippines to know these ghettos sometimes consisted of cardboard boxes or abandoned one room sheds that served as kitchen, bedroom and living quarters for a family.

My Filipino friend was quick to straighten my room, empty trash cans, teach me snippets of Filipino jargon that would help me navigate a local shopping mall and help me understand the currency exchange from dollars to pesos. On one occasion, he rescued me from the approach of a wealthy foreign man in the lobby who had mistaken me for a prostitute because of where I was sitting! So, it was without hesitation that I would retrieve my thrown-away belt for him. "It would fit my sister, Miss Monica. If you no longer need it, I will take it for you," he asked in broken English. I felt embarrassed at having thrown it away and, before we would say our goodbyes, I would provide him with various shirts, a pair of shoes, American chocolates and even a couple books I had in my suitcase.

I was under no illusion that my small gestures of kindness could change the folly that had enveloped this country, but as I had come to know at some point in the destination of my 20's, such crumbs of mercy do change hearts and impact lives, even if only for a day. My month's stay in the Philippines would change my worldview. They knew starvation and suffering the way I knew TV and strip malls. They sang songs in a sweaty bus ride through a smog infested city and smiled while children walked on the beach looking for food. They sang songs when I would be crying, they laughed when I would be yelling, they relished moments of convenience, and I complained about lines at Starbucks.

I returned to America, my fervor for serving others heightened. I would continue to assist patients and families dealing with CFIDS, FMS, and other chronic disorders as I had been doing for over two years, but now with a deeper awareness of the depth of suffering stretched across the canvas that is our world.

"We cannot do great things on this earth. We can only do small things with great love." Mother Teresa

Jesus spent much of his adult life without luxury or convenience. He knew his mission before others could even begin to understand it. He wasn't fazed by human stature or impressed by human wealth. In fact, he was drawn to the weak, the lonely and afraid: the mother who lost her child, the child who lost a limb, the man in politics who had acquired a bad reputation, the sick and the dying, the prostitute and the widow. Defeat didn't overcome him, and the massive sight of those who were lost didn't discourage his efforts. He knew his mission, clear in his purpose that service and sacrifice was not a destination but a way of life. The legacy he leaves, the spirit he wants us to cling boldly to, is a movement of our hearts beyond ourselves, a glimpse into the very definition of love.

Service became a driving force in my life—the roadmap uncertain but serving had become my compass. So, I began in my early 20's to rely on my instinct in approaching avenues of service and advocacy. I responded to this call without hesitation when I began a support group for patients suffering from Chronic Fatigue Syndrome (CFIDS), Fibromyalgia (FMS) and related chronic disorders.

I was 22 years old and had just graduated from college with a clear plan. First, find an apartment I could afford that was close to a grocery store and bank, get a kitten once the spring influx of unwanted litters filled up the local animal shelter and, lastly, start a support group. The first two tasks seemed effortless compared to the third. But within five months of graduating, I had secured a local meeting place, hung yellow cardstock signs throughout the city and gathered enough gumption buried deep under my timid and melancholy nature to make a go of it!

Before my first meeting, I wanted to collect any information on programs to assist patients and families that were available through hospitals or clinics. The response I got was one of ignorance and irritation. A local infectious disease doctor concluded that because he wasn't familiar with the conditions himself, they must not be 'real.' My efforts were futile, he informed me. Other doctors, physical therapists, chiropractors and even psychologists dismissed my efforts, their ignorance rampant and discouraging. A few months into my search, I would come across a patient in her 50's who had enough courage years before I did to organize a small gathering of patients in her home for bi-monthly meetings. The demands of the illnesses and unpredictability of patient attendance made her eager to pass along the information she had acquired.

Though discouraged by doctors, I was encouraged by a three-page list of fellow patients in need and began making plans for outreach. There is a stigma created by many who have *not walked in their shoes*, expressed through ignorance and a lack of sympathy. So, I knew I needed to approach patients not as people who needed me to fix them, but as a fellow patient who wanted to serve them.

I began advertising with local health facilities, radio stations and even help lines. I pinned yellow cardstock posters highlighting the location, time and date of our first meeting to bulletin boards at several food stores, all in an attempt to get the word out and fill the space I had reserved for our first meeting at a local wellness center.

A word came to me in secret, a mere whisper of a word, but I heard it. I had no choice except to surrender to it—the voice was one of peace and clarity of purpose...

It was the night of my second meeting as I walked out into the parking lot after 4 hours of working with patients. I drove home in a borrowed car to my tiny efficiency apartment on the outskirts of downtown. I slouched down in my yard-sale-lime-green couch as my new kitten climbed to perch on my shoulder and I smiled in satisfaction. Piles of meeting ideas covered my tiny kitchen table, patients' needs written on scraps of paper and left on phone messages, but they would remain there for now. I was overcome with a need to sleep 10 hours; after all, I was a patient myself. I would continue this work for close to a decade, learning the ebb and flow of serving chronically ill patients and, often, discouraged families.

The first meeting had close to 20 patients in attendance and over the subsequent years monthly meetings had a range of 10 to 40 patients and family members looking for support. The patients were welcomed in the room with a greeting table stacked with name tags, sign in sheets, and snacks I would make for each meeting. Early on, I regularly asked patients and family members what their most dire needs were. How could I best serve them? Responses ranged from recommending a doctor who understood CFIDS and FMS to any literature that would explain the illnesses to their spouses and co-workers. Some came with the expectation of socializing with like-minded sufferers, while others came in anticipation of a local speaker, they hoped would bring relief.

Most patients, however, came with one purpose in mind—absent of a cure, they wanted to learn about remedies that would bring a reprieve from symptoms. The weeks in between meetings, I would spend preparing a varied schedule of topics, a speaker every three to four months and materials to provide each patient with at meetings. I pieced together subject materials gathered from national organizations, magazines, books and various medical professionals I had begun to know in Sioux Falls. A sampling of topics included: alternative treatments for pain, time management, sleep disturbances, goals for life outside of suffering, how to cope with rejection from family, friends and strangers, the latest research, sufferers across the globe, advocating for further research, medications, nutrition, illnesses that accompany CFIDS and FMS, acceptance, finances, and effects on spouses and children.

Some patients couldn't attend meetings due to the intensity of symptoms, so I would go to their homes or mail them copies of any information I was providing. As my patient quota increased, so did the curiosity of local physicians—many still uncertain how to treat patients were becoming interested in trying.

On more than one occasion I would regret allowing a physician to speak at a meeting. My impressions of these doctors were that they seemed to be hiding a darker intention—their boasts of a cure in the form of intense exercise and sleeping pills or even, on one occasion, a doctor's desire to waste an hour of my patients time by dismissing CFIDS and FMS as made-up illnesses altogether, left me cleaning up their ignorant mess through reassuring phone calls to patients.

My journey became personal, my heart began to change, and while my social life became all but lonely, I found solace in these sufferers. I saw patients through divorces, births and even funerals. And every November I'd host a potluck for patients and their families as we gathered to give thanks for challenges that had brought us together.

"Whereas, the CFIDS/FMS Support Group in Sioux Falls joins The CFIDS Association of America and The National Fibromyalgia Association in observing May 12th, 2004, as Chronic Fatigue and Immune Dysfunction Syndrome and Fibromyalgia Syndrome Awareness Day." Mayor Dave Munson

I splashed water on my face after a two-hour nap, put on red lipstick, raced to put on the black high heels I had recently bought on clearance at Payless Shoes and hurried out my basement, efficiency apartment. Exactly three years after our first meeting, I would stand side by side with Mayor Dave Munson as he declared a proclamation in the city of Sioux Falls. He read the page-long proclamation to the city council and the patients and families who attended. The rest of the audience consisted of about 40 concerned citizens eager to bring attention to the streets filled with potholes, building permits needed on the south side of town, and the election of a new council official. And while he leaned in my direction for assistance in pronouncing the names of the illnesses, he effortlessly emphasized the most important paragraph—"Whereas, it is imperative that education and training of health professionals regarding CFIDS and FMS be expanded and that there be a greater public awareness of these serious health problems."

The proclamation remains in a slightly cracked skinny frame to this day, a reminder of the awareness that was a necessary component in increased advocacy and research. During the first few years, I would consult with the national support and research groups, stay apprised of the latest grassroots and governmental projects and do two local evening news reports. But it was working with patients and their families that would be my ultimate ambition.

Most of the group's expenses were funded through donations and my wallet, but as patient needs grew so did the financial demands. Months after the proclamation was announced, I was approached by a local businessman and lawyer whose father was battling FMS. He encouraged me to write a grant proposal to gain both financial assistance and medical networking. My first draft was a conservative and frugal attempt at maintaining the needs I currently had. It was quickly thrown out as I allowed myself to envision workshops, more sophisticated education materials and outreach to physicians, schools, and towns in the tri-state area.

I purchased a gray pin-striped business suit on clearance and wobbly black heels. My hands were sweaty and shaking as I got out of the elevator and entered a board room filled with four well-established hospital leaders—two of whom were physicians. Small talk gave way to distracted looks as I laid out my proposal and request for partnership and financial support. It was evident to me halfway through the presentation as chairs shuffled and cell phones were glanced at, that they had no desire to partner with me. I began to plan my exit. I turned down an offer from these hospital employees to "take over" my group.

Leaving both discouraged and hopeful, I continued to share plans for expansion and partnership with others. Within months, I received word from the competing hospital in town that a grant is offered each year to local projects and that I might be considered. Again, I presented my proposal, but this time to a one-person audience—a man greatly interested in funding grassroots opportunities. I shook his hand in disbelief, leaving his office with a smile and guarantee of assistance. This grant brought further outreach expanding the title and purpose beyond The CFIDS/FMS Support Group to 'The Support Network'—an organization focused on meetings and patient needs but also spreading outreach and awareness to the community of Sioux Falls and throughout the tri-state region (South Dakota, Minnesota and Iowa).

These funds allowed me to provide local school nurses with information on the diseases for serving both the needs of a possible student diagnosis or a family member of a student that had been diagnosed. From the beginning, I had invited both patients and their families to meetings. Being diagnosed as an adolescent, I knew firsthand how hard the journey from diagnosis through treatment can be for a family. For years my singular and greatest support was my mother. So, it became my primary goal upon meeting each patient to provide them with the assurance that they were not alone!

Before the formation of The Support Network, I had assisted two nurses in northwest Iowa in starting up a support group of their own. The 45-minute drive to Sioux Falls to attend monthly meetings was proving difficult for them since they were fellow patients and citizens of the Midwest winters. Now I was able to support them further, arranging for them to hold meetings at a medical clinic in their town, sending copies of recent monthly meeting topics and providing them with the most updated literature on FMS and CFIDS. They would come to a meeting in Sioux Falls a year later with a unique gift basket for me—in thanks for helping them start up a much-needed network of support for patients and families in their area. With the financial backing of the grant, I was able to further assist in the formation of a group in Watertown, SD and a small town between Chamberlain and Pierre.

As the patients increased, so did my outreach to local doctors and clinics. I was discouraged at the lack of willingness by some physicians to educate themselves on how to treat these patients. But would find solace in those who were willing to take a risk with my patients and me—many of them still assisting patients I sent to them 10 or even 15 years ago. Within five years I accumulated a referral list of a few primary care physicians, a chiropractor, a physical therapist, a neurologist and a psychologist that was readily available for patients looking for diagnosis and treatment. There were medical professionals willing to take referrals and some even willing to come speak at meetings. But only one, a physical therapist, treated my patients like people, not a problem to solve. Never in a hurry, he would greet them with a greater regard for their quality of life than his paycheck or patient quota. As the years passed and available treatments progressed, I brought in speakers, ran small clinics, and maintained a steady referral base for new patient arrivals.

Some people came for only one meeting, encouraged by the realization that their symptoms paled in comparison to those who couldn't work or those who had lost marriages and relationships with their children and friends. Others marched in the door determined to convince us of the cure they found in the form of some vitamin/mineral combination, medication or diet compilation—if only we'd fork over our often-diminished income to support their cause, we'd find rest from our ailments!

I didn't need a paycheck to know this was my job. My 'boss' was the fluctuating-yet-ever-present list of patient needs that sought my unwavering attention. These patients came to me in vulnerability and hope, and I wouldn't disappoint them.

Barbara was my first patient, a woman in her 60's whose husband never quite "got it." Her steady presence at the majority of meetings for close to a decade was a constant encouragement to me. She would advertise our meetings in her church bulletin and bring snacks to share with patients when she felt up to it. My faithful married-couple patients were Curt and DeVona. They both dealt with various diagnoses that led their immune systems to a weakened state leaving them with the ongoing symptoms of FMS. I'd laugh at Curt's jokes and hug DeVona when it didn't hurt, trying all the while to help them find treatments that eased their suffering. After seven years, I would say a tearful goodbye to DeVona after her painful and abrupt death from cancer.

There was a middle-aged woman who worked at a home improvement store. She often came in jeans and flannel, her tired eyes speaking more than she had the energy to do with words. Her husband would accompany her on occasion and every time he did, he would beg me to help her figure out a different coping technique. Her attempt at managing symptoms wasn't going well. She'd work 40 hours in four days and then stay bedridden in their home for the other three days each week. As a patient, I understood her desire to feel still functional and productive, but her husband's request was something I couldn't deny—he wanted a quality of life with his wife.

Pam would be my most jubilant of patients, she was a tall full-figured redhead, her symptoms of discomfort apparent, but her smile so much more infectious! One cold evening, she and her boyfriend showed up at my apartment in need of any financial assistance I could provide. Living in a basement efficiency, getting around town in taxis and running a support group on donations, I didn't have a lot to spare, but I wouldn't leave her emptyhanded. I took what I had from my wallet and provided them with some fruit and a dessert I had just made.

About three years into leading the group, I met a mother who was in a near-death grip as she fearlessly defended her adolescent son Michael against a disbelieving husband, ignorant doctors and an uninformed school system in a suburban town just outside of Sioux Falls. For two years, I would advocate for her son's welfare. Her husband remained unwilling to express support to his son with a difficult diagnosis. So, I would focus my efforts on finding treatments that would bring the patient relief—including medications, massage, counseling and alternative therapies. I was also called upon on more than one occasion as we met with teachers, faculty and the principle to develop an IEP (independent education program) that would suit his needs. Much like I had, he experienced weeks and months when he was unable to attend school.

I would assist in starting three other groups in smaller towns in South Dakota and Iowa and in almost a decade I would serve close to 200 patients and families. I was blessed by countless lives, encouraged by their endurance and stories and humbled by their belief in me. So, it came as a surprise when I knew with the same certainty with which I started the program that I would need to transition to another area of service—becoming your teacher.

"What matters is not the duration of your life, but the donation of it. Not how long you lived but how you lived." Rick Warren

As a mother away from any family support, I was already on call 24 hours a day, taking on the needs of you as an infant, toddler, and young child, which took much of my limited energy on most days. As you grew, however, I realized my energy distribution had to be redistributed to add teaching.

Mothers in many ways are already teachers—spending their days preparing, cleaning, instilling manners and morality, shaping a young heart through creative discipline and praise. But our journey as a home-schooling mother and child would require my attention to detail and the first fruits of my energy as you increased in knowledge and abilities. So, I surrendered to it, throwing myself upon it with the same fervor I once held in advocating for patients. I began research first into a preschool curriculum, then with each school year approaching I designed a routine and method to teaching, mothering, resting and finding new avenues of service for us both.

The call to become a home-schooling mother came unexpectedly but also with a great clarity of purpose. Having done the necessary research on Sioux Falls home school co-ops, activities, and education requirements, I began to peer into the dynamics of other home-schooling families. What did it look like? Were these children strangely different than their public-school counterparts? I knew instantly after meeting various families that I, too, would cherish the bond they seemed to have developed as a result of the journey with their children—all of whom seemed rather normal!

I never doubted my qualifications to teach. I had tutored various children over the years, spent months "teaching myself" while maintaining an above average GPA, and the skill set required to run The Support Network had given me a foundation for becoming a teacher. I also knew the reasons why I wanted to enter the world of home schooling. I didn't doubt the public-school system's ability to give an education experience, but I wanted to teach you something else that a strict 7-hour-a-day public school routine couldn't give you.

While our home became a classroom setting, you would learn in environments beyond our four walls. You learned math at the grocery and hardware stores, science in our backyard and the nearby ponds and lakes and, in the warmer months, you read and practiced spelling on the front porch. While your classroom lacked the constant commotion of other children, I scheduled weekly times with friends of varying ages, art, music and dance classes with your peers and camps in your areas of interest each summer. And I took a nannying job for a family that welcomed us *both* into their home and lives for much of your childhood.

"What is most important and valuable about the home as a base for children's growth into the world is not that it is a better school than the schools, but that it isn't a school at all." John Holt

Every mother wants her child to have the best education and opportunities she can provide. There was something else I wanted for you even more. The public-school structure highlights the intense competition of intellectual and social norms. Grades are not a reflection of how well the teacher explains a concept but mostly how *fast* the child learns. Students are instantly put into peer groups based on their abilities in sports, academia, and popularity. And while years are spent experiencing 'normal' childhood memories of classroom parties and fading crushes, I wanted you to experience more. Becoming your teacher was my journey—learning without boundaries would be yours.

If there was one thing, I hoped you would gain from your home-schooling experience, it was that learning should be a way of life—not a destination. I re-enforced concepts until you complained they had become too easy, but I didn't give you a letter grade for subjects until high school. I wanted you to discover that learning multiplication, all the bones in a hand or how to write a thesis was an opportunity, not just a letter grade to acquire.

Of course, being a bookworm myself, I loved the idea of learning even more than I enjoyed teaching. So, our journey was shared as I learned right beside you about the great white shark and the early settlers that I somehow misplaced in the years since 2nd grade. I would re-enter high school when you learned algebra and spend hours studying concepts, I hoped you would retain. But more than knowledge, more than high standardized test scores, I wanted you to develop a lifestyle of learning that was integrated with lessons on character.

If I had taught you to read, write and memorize the history of the 19th century but I didn't teach you how to show compassion for those in need, I would have left out the most important subject. If you knew how to use a computer and read a grade ahead of your peers, but you didn't know appreciation, humility or a resolute approach to life's hardships I would have failed as your teacher. Luckily, you were born with a spirit of unyielding joy which made my task much easier.

The greatest benefit of home schooling, I would notice early, was the ability to teach and learn in the context of serving. I transitioned from advocating for patients to teaching you and my purpose of serving became ours as I mapped out areas of interest for a young child. In your preschool years, I would take you to parks in the poorest sections of Sioux Falls and encourage you to bless the other kids and on occasion, you gave the stuffed toy or purse you had brought with you to a girl with tattered clothes or lonely eyes. And in all your 'playground years' you would seek out the children in need of a friend. No matter their age, you sought to bless them through play.

Before the age of 7, you had multiple surgeries; a routine tonsillectomy required a week's recovery in the hospital and numerous eye surgeries were performed to remove tumors that had grown in the tear ducts of your eyes. Even at this young age, you began to extend your compassion for the children you saw sitting in fear at appointments and before surgery. On your 4th birthday, you would appear on a local TV news telethon that was highlighting the local Children's Hospital's need for donations to children. And that began my yearly request for you to 'give' on or around your birthday. It wasn't surprising that you often picked animals to give to and on more than one year we took donations to the local animal shelter to celebrate all that you had been given on your birthday.

You are a gift, and God deserved my thanks. It seems foolish to think I would have anything of value to offer such a gracious God; yet I knew with certainty that I wanted you to know him. Religion is haunting in its ability to turn a relationship into a rule system, but I wanted you to know the God I had come to know, and so I went to the place he is worshiped – church. Together you and I would serve in various capacities; caring for infants whose parents wanted to attend service without interruption, delivering meals to families that had a recent birth or death, serving potlucks and welcoming newcomers.

Each Thanksgiving or Christmas season I would ask you who we should bless. Together we would carry out our 'baskets of blessing' or gifts you had made for our bank employees, neighbors, the homeless, kids in need or store clerks. You would climb in the car, eventually old enough to ride in the front seat, and we would make our deliveries.

Your conception had made me your mother. Our home school lifestyle had made me your teacher. It was through our shared experience of looking in the eyes of those in need that we became friends. And together, we gathered the riches of serving others.

Chapter 3 – Cul-de-Sac Roots

"The great thing about getting older is you don't lose all the other ages you've been." Madeleine L' Engle

My child,

I was a daughter, a sister and a woman before you were born. But first, I was a child...

I was born and raised in the California valley where smog and sun collide, and strip malls scatter the landscape. I lived the childhood that I can remember, starting at age 5, in a quaint and quiet cul-de-sac called Potts Court in the Sacramento Valley.

It was the 1980s. Cyndi Lauper and Michael Jackson played in our boom boxes, Dan Rather delivered the 6 o'clock evening news and high perms, neon leg warmers and pink eye shadow were the latest fashion trends.

Your grandfather was a 'house flipper,' years before the term was popularized by mainstream cable T.V. and so all around my kiddy pool was dirt. Lots and lots of dirt. A fence separated the yards, as is common in the suburban landscape of California, but even in those first memories of that home I remember the vastness I felt surrounded by our half acre lot. My dad would do much of the redesign on the house and yard. And my mother was the keeper of the progress— pridefully pulling the bulking photo albums from the bookshelf to show guests all the work that had been done. We had a German neighbor to the north who had an algae filled pool in her backyard and an older couple to the south who would give us painted ceramics or hand crafted dolls each holiday. Other neighbors filled the cul-de-sac—some who would move and others I never knew well. But the steadfast presence of one family, the Edwards, would prove to be life altering for our family of four. Over the decades their status grew beyond neighbors with a spare key or friends on the Fourth of July—they had filled the role of second parents to me—so entwined in each other's emotions and memories we had become family without even knowing it.

"Love can build a bridge, between your heart and mine. Love can build a bridge, don't you think it's time?
Don't you think it's time?..."
The Judd's "Love Can Build a Bridge"

My sister and I were roommates until I was 11 years old and she remained my envy for years beyond that. I was certain that in our three-year age difference your aunt had acquired all the wisdom I was lacking. Our room decorated in 1980's country motif, much like the rest of our house, was your grandmother's canvas—her love affair with all shades of blue.

When we were young, your grandmother dressed us in different, yet complementary colors for every holiday, birthday and milestone that gave her an excuse to hold a camera. The leather-bound albums served as visual growth charts and maps to changing clothing and hair styles. So, I followed her each morning into our shared bathroom eager for her to do my hair, paint my nails or let me borrow her bright pink lipstick when mom wasn't looking. On occasion, I would sneak into her closet and try on her clothes. (This habit continued long into my teen years unbeknownst to her.)

One of my favorite memories with my sister was singing and laughing while we did our hair each morning. While she enjoyed Madonna and The Pointer Sisters, I was preferred Tears For Fears, Randy Travis and Cyndi Lauper.

For Christmas a few years ago, I made her a mix-CD, modern songs by Justin Timberlake and a recent children's movie soundtrack. I couldn't refrain from adding a few songs from our childhood. The intro to the evening show "Golden Girls" and *"Love Can Build a Bridge"* a song by The Judds. I played the CD for you in the car before sending it to my sister. I shared with you how when I was your age, my sister and I would bellow these songs out in failed tune, rushing from our bathroom performance to rewind our cassette tape. We were each other's audience, greatest fan and in natural sibling order she took on the role of bodyguard.

It was 3rd grade. I was in tears after a girl from an adjoining classroom had accused me of lying. I knew my safe place would be with my sister, as we walked home together from our shared elementary school. My tears slowed, and the fear and embarrassment subsided with her presence. She maintained her eagle like stature over me, even on the occasions I don't recall asking her to.

My sister was to become highly respected for her leadership

skills—a strong "type A" personality, both in high school and the years to follow. Her success never surprised me. She always exuded a natural tendency to delegate and create.

Our sibling status is divided by many miles now. She's spent decades working at a prestigious financial firm. The bustling city is her oasis as she arrives home to a husband of immense integrity and two Nike-dressed children who echo her humor and strength.

My sister and I infiltrate one other's lives where blood and memories bond us together. And yet, we remain separated by miles and personality. I live in my head, addicted to the written word, content to spend hours or days without interacting with anyone. My sister enters every door with a smile and determination to always see the good. I am vulnerable, she is stoic. She has season tickets to her favorite sports team, I get to the book store before it opens and prefer watching flowers grow to standing in a crowd. And while I stand 5 inches taller than her, I am smaller still. I will sit on a stool in front of her as she straightens my hair, even now as we approach our 40's. Her petite hands, brightly painted nails and rings to match her day's style, run through my curls and we are children again. After each sparsely scattered visit I am reminded of the pull that keeps us close and yet far apart. The prairie is my home, not from blood or marriage, but my soul's finding of peace. Somewhere in the days turned to years, I developed a confidence I struggled to find as a child, a feeling of comfort in my own sickly skin.

As we parted ways during my last visit to the Sacramento Valley, we hugged as you were squeezed between us. I sobbed, you joined in and my sister's eyes spoke a tenderness that opened a window to her heart, the place behind the strength she holds so tightly. She said she was proud of me—her words covered my insecurities. Her strength as a child was due in part from her personality and part from sibling order. I am not sure if she ever wanted to be the younger sibling, but there are times in my adult years that I wished I was no longer the 'younger sister.' As I'd like to think, that somehow, I've caught up with the experiences and wisdom the three-year gap left.

"...I realize that photos also distort what is really being captured. To get the best shot, the messiness is shoved to the side, the weedy yard is out of the shot." - Amy Tan

I had a common childhood, wrapped in the security of suburbia, with parents whose loyalty to the idea of marriage, family and morality kept us whole. But this is not to be confused with perfection, for our suburban routine was checkered with ghosts of an adult world I couldn't comprehend as a young girl. Both of my parents were not just my parents—they were individuals with their own insecurities, regrets and expectations. Although, as a child, I was convinced they existed purely to serve and entertain me. Yet, it didn't keep me from questions, emotional scars and baggage I would have to open and sort through as an adult.

Those early years were sprinkled with roots and routine. If my father bestowed identity, then my mother sought to convey a sense of self-worth. Your grandmother, an Irish Catholic conservative, saw to it that we followed the moral code of the religious middle class. We were baptized, confirmed and given a list of weekly chores all in an attempt to keep us both morally erect and humble.

While your grandmother worked as a full-time bookkeeper for decades, her more profound role came as the caretaker of our home. Every season she redecorated the house, each holiday she had pictures to take, cookies to bake, cards to send and traditions to repeat. And in her painstaking devotion to detail she even took time to write notes on our napkins, so we'd have something special to read at lunch each day at school.

Your grandmother, the image of tradition, was always found in my childhood engaged in some sort of preparation—whether it was the anticipation of a holiday, religious milestone, Sunday afternoon ironing or Tuesday night pork chops. She was never found relaxing in a lazy boy chair with her feet up. I would wrestle with this example in my growing years and adulthood, as I craved the company of literature and art, sleeping till 10am, playing with animals, sipping wine and debating topics taboo to our conservative way. But for a time, I simply thought my mother needed to relax.

As a teenager I pleaded with her to forgo the dishes in exchange for an evening of fun. I was humored with a nod as though in my young years I had yet to grasp the realities of adult responsibility.

Eventually I saw that she knew her joy all along in the form of shopping malls and preparing for the next occasion of fellowship with family and friends. And all that responsibility that kept her from evenings of play was my ignorance, for I came to know all too well the demands of adulthood and motherhood with your arrival in my life. My mother captured the essence of the 'mom job'—throwing herself into it, never being undone by the pressure of its demands. Ultimately, it would be this grace and patience that I sought to portray as I became a mother myself.

My father was just as you now know him, full of energy and eagerness. He's a salesman, in nature and vocation. Without effort, his enthusiasm is infectious and influencing. Throughout my childhood, my image of him was one of reverence and curiosity. He was always 'doing something.' The never-ending maintenance of our home and the mechanical and building-projects that surrounded us always had his attention. Never wavering in his desire to provide for our family his hard work ethic is seen mirrored in my sister to this day. But it wouldn't be until I was an adult that I began to see my father beyond his role as my dad. If my mother would 'prepare' in her attempts to demonstrate her love, my father would be the one to 'fix.'

After you were born, I began to seek his counsel in his areas of expertise – cars, building, salesmanship and barbecuing, among others. After moving to the Midwest at age 18, I never returned to California to make a home, but every trip back an opportunity for me to immerse myself in the wisdom of my parents' experiences, their histories, their legacies.

"...I can never escape the world where I am from." – Melanie Hoffert

On one of my trips back to California you were toddling around your great grandparents, Grandma 'Mary' and Grandpa Calvin's, house. My father and I were going through sheds, rooms and cupboards that were saturated with memories from his childhood and mine. I had heard repeated stories in my youth of my father's love affair with animals including dogs, cats, rabbits, horses and his prized pigeon collection.

There were memories of my early years reflected in the rooms of my grandparent's home—the old yellow chair my grandmother sat in as she watched us open gifts, china that was used each Thanksgiving, linens frayed just slightly at the edges from decades of use, rustic kitchen cupboards that for many years I never opened because I was too short. And the secret garden Grandma Mary kept. It was a hidden oasis. It took up more than half of the backyard, bordered by a tall dark wood fence my cousins and I would peer through as children. As a child I imagined the space beyond the raggedy fencing contained garden fairies that delivered all the pumpkins, squash, green beans, corn and peas that appeared fresh on our Thanksgiving table each year. I envied my grandmother, even when I was young, the way she seemed almost lost in the landscape, that she and my grandfather had built so many years before. Her hands were always dirty and her lipstick always red, her hair in a bun and her stature always ready to serve and welcome you back.

When I was home from college one Christmas break, I had a life-altering conversation with my grandmother. In my parent's kitchen with no one else home, she confided to me in a matter of fact tone that she was dying. Most likely, but not discussed formally, was the effect alcohol had on her organs. It would be close to a decade before she passed, but she knew even then that she was living on borrowed time.

My grandmother battled alcoholism for much of her adult life. This dark place is inside the soul of everyone—the place where life and fear meet, and insecurities and habits get entangled. Her pain, though, became a teacher. Her weakness became a way for me to understand the power our habits have over our spirits and their sphere of influence over those around us.

Time erodes the accuracy of images
while evoking the distant emotions

I was 10 years old, and my sister and I went to spend a week with my grandparents. Days were filled with playing games and planning performances with two girl cousins, the same age as us. We enjoyed Teddy, the small, dirty, white mutt that followed my grandfather around and annoyed my grandma as he darted between her legs. But more than anything, I remember the food. On a small wobbly wooden table my grandparents sat with their coffee and wine, their cigarettes and newspapers the centerpiece. It was here we would sit for breakfasts and lunches. Grandma Mary always had the best food; chocolate milk, Cheetos, ice cream and cookies. Suppers were different though; they were delicious spreads of chicken or beef with fresh garden veggies. I became smitten with her green beans, corn on the cob and fried zucchini. Yet, on this particular visit, my sister and

I would experience wrath hidden under grandmother's welcoming demeanor. Looking back, I imagine she felt emotions of frustration that she tried to hide by noon each day with wine. She was crying out for help, but no one knew what to do so they turned their heads. But at the time, all I felt was hurt at her demeaning words, declaring that my sister and I were lazy and ungrateful because she was serving us while we were watching a movie with my grandfather. She threatened to tell our parents, but my mother never heard anything from her, only our pained retelling of the story. My mother hugged us, aware of something we couldn't yet fully understand—the unpredictable nature of alcoholism.

This crutch in my grandmother's life—the dark habit she would return to over and over again was something I was aware of, but never defined my perception of her. She was in my mind, Mother Earth, Betty Crocker and Mother Teresa all in one! She had fearlessness *and* an alcohol tendency she passed down both to some of her children, including my father. And while a wine glass was always close to her hand, her heart belonged to the Lord. She gave so many of her years to giving to those in need—a nearby hospital, her church, neighbors, children and grandchildren and her closest companion—my grandfather—whom she cared for until her death.

Days before she passed, we talked on the phone. Many miles separated us and we hadn't hugged in a couple years, but I needed her to know how much I loved her and how assured I was that she would be greeted by a merciful and loving God. I needed her to know with my words that I saw her, and I was blessed by her for 31 years. And that fateful day in my parent's kitchen, on break from my new life in the prairie, I felt a spiritual connection with your great grandmother that I carry with me even now as I dig in the dirt of my garden and help those in need.

If my paternal grandmother was a student of the land and heart, my maternal grandmother is a librarian and reporter. Not in the literal sense, but to anyone who knows her she is the keeper of records and current events. Her meticulous attention to detail allows her to relay dates, events and relatives you didn't know you wanted to know! Books of every genre line her antique shelves and Mozart and Beethoven echo through the walls of a home she has lived in for more than 60 years. At 94 years old, she is a shrinking German / Prussian descendant whose attention to detail has provided every child (6), grandchild (16) and great-grandchild (11 to date) with a quilt or two, books for lifelong learning and a legacy she and my grandfather retold for nearly 60 years together.

"The greatest generation was formed first by the Great Depression. They shared everything – meals, jobs, clothing." Tom Brokaw

My maternal grandparents, Iola and Maurice met in San Francisco, CA in 1947 and married in September 1948. My grandpa was stationed there in the navy after serving on the USS Escambia AO8O and spending over three years in the South Pacific. My grandma had moved there with a girlfriend in the summer of 1947 after leaving her family and a job working for the mayor of Aberdeen in South Dakota.

My grandmother left the north eastern part of South Dakota eagerly at age 21 with a curious mind for the world outside of farming and temperatures above freezing. My grandfather left the Dakotas out of duty to his country and after marrying at 23 years old, he assumed he and his bride would return. Their compromise was a yearly trip returning to their roots, which they continued until two years before my grandfather passed away.

Like many people, in tracing the lineage of my family I stumble upon surprises. A 1% Indian (Asian) ethnicity or the unconfirmed claim that one of my ancestors was the Prince of Orange. The distant is made familiar through pictures of my maternal great-grandmother, Anna. She looks just like my mother and the same glimmer in their eyes can be found in the fullness of yours. I find it curious how my passion for words, animals and the untamed land were handed down without guidance from my grandmothers, as though a genetic mutation seeped into the blood line. Even more than genetic similarities, I see a persistent theme of fearlessness in both branches of my family tree. The distant ancestors experienced the grave impact of job loss in one-income households, consecutive world wars and the wretched pain from deaths of children due to incurable diseases. They were unaware of the surplus and advancements that would come with future generations, but understood and embraced the timeless hallmarks of love, hard work, morality and honesty. They are a generation defined by loss and their ability to rise from it stronger and wiser.

"When you get to the corner…," my grandpa said, "…turn!"

Navy officer pictures of him tell stories lost to time and war, but most of his stories were filled with humor and mischief. He'd rise from his lazy boy chair to walk us out to our cars, give us a hug and kiss and remind us to smile with a plethora of riddles and jokes. Maurice's mother Anna died when her children were young and my grandfather and his siblings were put in multiple orphanages by his father, 'Pop,' whose cowboy tendencies made it hard to support the needs of his 7 remaining children. In the town of Montrose, SD (not too far from where you are growing up) there are headstones of your 2nd great grandparents. There is an auctioned land parcel, a prairie treasure map, that holds clues of his childhood found hidden in farmers' backyards.

I was 26 years old, the last time I saw my grandfather. He and my grandma had made their yearly trip to South Dakota to visit remaining family and friends. They stopped in Sioux Falls on a Monday and took me out to lunch at Perkins Restaurant. My grandfather drove us back to my tiny efficiency apartment where my grandpa took a nap and my grandma informed me that 'he wasn't doing too well.' Grandpa awoke from his nap, exchanged pleasantries and left with a hug and kiss. He handed me a wad of cash as he always had when he visited and reminded me that where I had found home (South Dakota), was and always would be "God's country."

I can still feel the warmth of his lips on my cheek, and comfort of his embrace. I miss him dearly but am comforted by the fact that you know the same attributes as my beloved grandfather. Your father greets you each day with his all-encompassing hugs, he relays and repeats history of the Sioux Falls area like only a grandfather can, and every time he smiles at you, I think of the joy that covered my grandfather's face when one of his children or grandchildren entered the room.

I think of the fearlessness of earlier travelers who faced threats and hardships in their search for a free and prosperous settlement. Were they captivated by the sheer magnificence of wide-open space and the lure of the unknown? Did sadness over what would be left behind keep them from wandering? Are we not fighting the same battle of complacency, contentment and desire for more in our modern age?

According to a mail-order testing kit I am forty-five percent Irish. This confirms the stories told to me by my maternal grandfather about ancestors that came from Ireland to escape the poverty of the potato famine. Other lines can be traced back to a few western European countries including lands formerly referred to as Holland and Prussia. These lines intersected and created the majestic family tree we are part of. The beauty of these roots, branches and twigs is found entwined in personal anecdotes, pursuits of love and fortune and the willingness to embrace the unknown.

A great painter studies and appreciates his creation. He isn't afraid to erase, soften or redefine the edges of penciled outlines in order to establish a finished masterpiece. In the same way, I suggest that you revisit what shaped you—the innocence of childhood, the roots and routines that sprinkled your early years. Don't mimic your past for the sake of tradition, though. Instead, gain discernment, laugh and rejoice at milestones. It will be a timeless teacher.

Chapter 4 – After Innocence

"It takes courage to grow up and become who you really are."
E.E. Cummings

My dearest daughter,

I was a statue on a 2-foot wooden stage, surrounded by artists who would make my pale, disease-stricken body seem full of radiant beauty on their worn canvases.

I walked the downtown streets, stopping to peer at a shop's window posting. An artist's facial sketch appeared beside the posting that read: *"Wanted: A female model for portrait drawings and paintings. Pay is $7.00 an hour."* I rang the bell and was greeted by two young artists eager to show me around the upstairs studios. The tall steep staircase opened to walls of framed acrylic-covered canvases, each one a story told in a frame. A room to the east was kept warm by a fireplace and decorated with antique furniture and floor-to-ceiling bookshelves regularly disheveled by the young apprentices seeking instruction *or* a muse. The main room was a place of study for students, still life drawings and caste-charcoal pages pinned to the darkened walls. The hallway to the west led to the artist's personal spaces lined with little inspirations and pieces apparently still being perfected. I answered the ad, posed for a portrait drawing and started a two decade's long career as a model.

After repeated portrait sessions, I was introduced to the husband and wife artist team that taught the eclectic and intimate group of students in the classical tradition of Old Masters such as Rembrandt, Vermeer, and Sargent. In the months to follow, I was asked to pose in full-nude form.

It was an autumn day; I remember because I felt a breeze seeping through the walls of the historic downtown studio even though the radiators were shaking in their efforts to keep us warm. The studio owner's wife was hosting my first pose in her personal studio space; she seemed both eager and nervous at my arrival. In broken English, she explained her idea for a pose, her vision for the piece—a woman propped against a wall, draped in a red robe, peering through a window in guarded contemplation. After weeks of modeling for her and a handful of students at the studio, I would begin to model for her husband Hans, the owner of the studio.

He was seductive with dark eyes and windblown hair (like a Stentson cologne commercial). I would succumb to his allure, as most would, if only for a time. His magnetism faded, giving way to mood swings and empty canvases.

The studio was filled with music, candles and romantic visions of the human form. I would be his muse—an 'angel vision' with feathered wings he would make first in pencil on a 4-foot canvas and sell at a gallery in Virginia.

"I need to know where my angel came from," spoke the buyer of the first piece of me ever sold. Hans would call me the night of the gallery show, asking for a mysterious back story he could relay to the curious buyer. We brainstormed a mix of fact and fiction—accenting the truth with a bit of flare. Hans would convey to the customer how

I traveled across the country alone at 18 years old to pursue education and art and that I had a strong Irish background which explained my pale skin and dark features. The buyer, a middle-aged businessman with an accent, seemed only partially satisfied with this tale as he stared into the dark eyes—now a muse on his wall.

My journey as a model would begin to expand beyond the owner Hans, his wife and their studio. Within a few years, I would follow one of those students, Anna Youngers, to her own studio as she began to establish herself as a well-known artist within Sioux Falls and the surrounding region. That friendship would become a lifelong treasure as she shared in many of the milestones of my adult years—including being there to hold you shortly after you were born. Annie formed my expectations for my modeling experiences. She welcomed me into her studio and her classes as one would a friend into their home. She was my gateway into the hearts and minds of artists that I would have otherwise never known.

"..Art brings us all the way into discipline…within those parameters, there is a world of free." Lisa-Jo Baker

While the first piece of me was hung and purchased in a gallery in Virginia, others would be bought and sold in galleries in Florida, Arizona, and South Dakota. Many others remain in the store house files of an artists' unfinished work. I would be a mermaid, a Middle Eastern woman wrapped in a turban, a peasant girl, a tropical vision wrapped in white cotton with a flower in my hair and a mother among many others. I would hold a globe, a flower, a book, a robe, a hat and sometimes nothing at all. Some artists would stay to draw in pencil for hours at a time; others were quick with their charcoal, leaving impressions on page after page—their fingers smearing the sharp corners of their figures.

In posing for multiple artists, each positioned at a slightly different angle from me, I would observe their unique glares—their apparent zeal at putting on paper what their impressions inspired them to create. I never felt naked, although sometimes I did get cold. My presence seemed to get lost in the imaginations of the artists who were creating more than a mere figure on a page.

Some assignments and poses were more challenging than others, the best ones left me in a raw and relaxed state. Still, others left me wishing I hadn't taken my clothes off at all! I would come to trust a few in the art community, anyone they brought in to draw me I knew would be just as respectful.

Still, there were two occasions in the decades of modeling when I felt uncomfortable and left the particular studio—never to return. I was 25 years old and had been invited to pose for a group of artists that met in the evenings once a week in a sprawling 3rd floor of an old barn building. About twelve adults of varying ages gathered in the cold and rustic building that was adjacent to a well-known college in Sioux Falls. As I closed the door to my red Mercury Topaz and entered the art center, I was ushered into an instructor's office to change into a robe. Instantly, I felt uncomfortable, but I couldn't put my finger on why. Shaking off what I assumed was just nerves, I posed for the group in both sitting and standing positions. The 'nerves' never left, and so after attending two sessions, I declined further invitations. In many ways, I felt like those in attendance were more concerned with mindless chatter among themselves than with creating a piece in tune with my presence.

I would feel the same stirring of misplacement in recent years when I agreed to pose for a local artist who had acquired studio space. It took me only one time posing in his studio with other artists present to feel as I had in the old barn years prior—out of tune with the artists that were present to draw me. In neither instance was I disrespected or harmed, but my intuition which has always served me well, guided me to the exit.

As a model I was, for all intents and purposes, a statue used to inspire artists to create and teach the human form. Even so, I had come to learn early on that a live model was in fact not a statue, but a living, breathing and feeling person. Often a live model's eyes would reflect the emotions and thoughts she had buried in her heart. Unbeknownst to many models, after ten minutes of posing the body begins to 'settle in' to a position with a hip moving slightly to the left or a wrist turning to reveal a bit more of the hand. An artist dedicated to the subject matter is aware of this and patiently waits to see what the pose reveals.

As a model, I wanted my artists to be pleased with my presence and to find inspiration in my pose. It wasn't about achieving perfection or sexuality—it was about expressing the innate beauty and tenderness of a woman's form. No matter the audience, a woman's mystery is found in all that she is—a pure child, a loving mother, a kind friend, or a generous lover. It is the reason we want to protect her when she's young and listen to her stories when she's old.

The pressure to maintain this satisfaction increased as I got older and more insecure about my aging appearance. Would the fundamental shifts of giving birth, acquiring wrinkles and stretch marks, leave my artists seeking other forms of inspiration? Much like a writer is inspired by poetry or a musician stirred by rhythm, I tried to be a catalyst to their creative process. The modeling experiences I have been most pleased with have been those where a certain amount of chemistry has given way to a relationship between the artist and myself. That *together* we are creating a vision to be enjoyed again and again—like a song replayed to ignite the soul's energy or comfort.

A local artist and professor, Scott Parsons, would be the first artist to give me a piece of his work freely. They are rolled together in my closet; wrinkles have found the edges over the last 15 years since he handed them to me. Two white pages of charcoal drawings—one a side view of my back, the other a front image of my torso and neck, signed by a man and artist I've come to admire. He would come to paint and to draw, but mostly he came to sketch charcoal drawings of me for hours at a time. His smile is shy and his laughter soft and infectious. A renowned professor at a local college, he would send some of his students to the studio to paint me and time and time again requested my presence to model for his classes.

I was six months pregnant with you when Annie started a painting of me that she never finished because you came unexpectedly, weeks before your due date. I was lying against pillows that were pushed discreetly between my limbs to create the defining beauty that is a pregnant woman. The weeks spent on this pose were effortless as the pain increased in my back due to your constant pushing. It almost didn't seem fair to get paid for lying down! We would laugh at your attempts to participate—the roundness of your head or poking of your arm would reveal itself as she glanced from subject to the canvas.

In recent years, a local doctor and his wife both active in support of local artists came upon a portrait of me leaning against the walls of Annie's studio. I was wearing a brown farmer's hat and maintained a look of confidence and wonder as I stared out the window of her studio for hours at a time. The unfinished painting sat in the corner of her studio several years incomplete and my lips and chin in need of more definition. From time to time Annie would revisit it, looking for inspiration and time to complete the piece—only to find it at the request of a local doctor and his wife. As she completed the painting, I spent the most gorgeous of autumn mornings with Annie, deep in the clutches of the doctor's land—a sprawling 100 acres to the east of Sioux Falls. My farmer's hat and a wool sweater in tow we hiked the area as the sun rose in search of the perfect prairie background for the piece of me that would hang in their home.

I envy the artists I have worked for, so passionate about their cause, so determined in their efforts to create, so sure of who they are! They create some pieces that are whimsical and gallery-worthy, others that you want hung in your entry way and others that leave you wanting more. I am challenged by the best of them to abandon my perfectionist tendencies and immerse myself in the pure joy of creating.

Move ahead in your weakness and do the right thing in spite of your fear and insecurities. It's then you'll begin to form your integrity.

"You need to be careful because men will see you and try things to get your attention," my mom whispered as we got into the car. She had come to visit me for a week at some point in my early 20's— staying with my new kitten and me in my three-room apartment. My mother, never one for words, was giving me the same speech, she delivered when I was six years old and learning about 'stranger danger.' I had been explicitly instructed to run when approached by strangers with puppies or candy who tried to lure me into their cars. I laughed off her warnings as I had no intention of getting into a car with a strange man no matter how cute his dog was, but in the months to follow I would begin to understand what she already knew. I was no longer a child; my innocence had slowly faded like paint on a high-gloss table.

People tend to cringe at the unknown or unusual; we form groups to solidify our political views, churches to affirm our faith and suburbs to keep in touch with the 'Joneses.' My choice to model was not met with unanimous applause, but I was never ashamed—my honor firmly intact.

My modeling career would do something that no other person had been able to do—it would make my sick body well if only in the eyes of an artist, if only in a wooden-framed canvas. In fact, I felt more at ease posing for respected artists than speaking in front of a crowd! I began to see a creator in the rawness and innocent beauty of the human form—the unrelenting attention to detail in the passion of some of the artists.

But it was then, in the owner's wife's studio, the day I posed for her and three art students that I realized my innocence had passed. Not because someone took it by force or even asked for it. I knew at that moment that I no longer saw myself or my world as a pure and fair safety net. I had become a woman, not because I turned a certain age or was granted the lawful right to vote or drink; I had become a woman because I realized I was no longer a child. And I knew then that my integrity, my notion of wholeness, would be solely determined by my choices.

Some define innocence as the hopeful and pure pouncing of the young—yet to be touched by shame or defiled by sexuality. My innocence was thankfully never forcefully taken from me, but I had released my grip on it slowly, making choices out of curiosity and confusion rather than an awareness of who I wanted to be. And my regrets live in the hollow pockets that separated my innocence from my unformed integrity.

My Catholic upbringing laid out the moral compass of right and wrong. I was given rules to follow and expectations to live up to. And at a young age I learned that some would encounter that which is unfair and unexplainable, they will struggle when others soar; they will know pain and loss while their peers are wrapped in childlike glee. I didn't know how to prioritize my Catholic roots and unexplainable medical diagnosis as a child. So, as my teenage years ended, confusion set in. And at 18 years old, I moved 2,000 miles away from family, friends and all I had ever known because I wanted to redefine my existence, although I wasn't completely sure what that was supposed to look like.

I had longed to be here—this place called adulthood. Arriving at this destination was expected to replace the loss and pain of my childhood diagnosis with an unambiguous freedom. Instead, I felt a mix of emotion—a concern for the pride I wanted my family so far away to feel for me and yet the need to experience it all on my own, far away from them in case I failed their expectations. I often wondered in my 20s whether I brought shame and embarrassment upon my family. How much easier it may have been to just stay living with my parents, using all those around as a crutch of comfort as I found my way through the trappings of the strip malls, interstates, and suburban landscape. If only I had done what was expected of me instead of what seemed to come naturally.

When I was 20 years old, I met a local nun in charge of a Catholic Family Services organization in Sioux Falls. She was my mentor, colleague, and friend for close to 8 years. Sister Mary Carole Curran would teach me how to advocate for those in pain, how serving isn't about numbers but about lives and how I needed to quiet my soul to hear the whisper of my purpose. She would tame my appetite for perfectionism with the reminder that a higher calling of service had been imprinted on my mind—my passion for art and serving those in need was an assignment I couldn't ignore.

I asked her once when she had felt the calling on her life to be celibate. She said in her late teens she had heard the whisper and while there were fleeting moments of doubt and fear in the early years of becoming a nun she knew with certainty; it was her savior that she was enamored with. By my adult years, I was no longer a practicing Catholic and I enjoyed sex too much to give it up, but I envied her apparent devotion, the reckless abandon to serve that she lived by.

She seemed utterly unfazed by hardship. "You can do two things with a pile of shit," she would say, "You can throw it against a wall and look at it *or* use it to plant flowers!" While I was startled to hear her use such words, she seemed equally unembarrassed by them. She would doze off when others gave speeches and somehow retain all that was said. Her silence often led me to believe she was bored or distracted. It took me a few years to discern that it was in her silence that she was fully present in my mind, ready with the obvious tidbit of wisdom that was always *less is more*. As I continued my modeling career and started a non-profit for patients and families, I carried with me her ability to reserve judgment and to counsel with unwavering compassion.

Sister Mary Carole was my Mother Teresa. She traveled to impoverished countries throughout the world to help the sick and poor, worked tirelessly to serve orphans, assisted families who experienced a death, a job loss, and anyone that came in her path— including the ongoing list of patients I would refer to her over the time we served together.

It would take me close to a decade before I began to know myself without the trappings of shame, loss or confusion and this clarity could not have been uncovered without the heart of one unfailing nun.

You gave me life itself and incredible love, You watched and guarded every breath I took, but you never told me about this part. I should have known that there was more to it.

Job 10: 12-13

Those early adult years were scattered with more fears than perspective. How I wish I could tell my younger self not to be led by other's expectations or the emotional high that comes with all that is new, but instead to be led by the peace that comes from knowing your purpose. Many nights during my first decade living in South Dakota, I cried myself to sleep in confusion and fear. The only thing I was certain of was that I couldn't go back to California and that the minimal and sundry existence I was embarking on was somehow beginning to feel like home.

My entrance from innocence to integrity was found somewhere in my 20's. I was disillusioned by religion—yet certain I knew God was present. I was disappointed by what I didn't get in my childhood and questioned what kind of purpose my life could serve in daily pain and unrelenting fatigue. I searched, tried on, ran from, and made choices from a place of loneliness that I would later regret. No one moment remade me and yet together they formed the legacy I now leave you.

When we are young we are surprised by life—gifts on Christmas morning, vacations to Disneyland, friends we can play hide and seek with, staying up late and eating cake for breakfast—all arranged by the adult figures in our lives. We are blissfully unaware that these adults have any purpose beyond our existence, so we surrender to their guidance and expectations. So, it's no surprise when we repeat their lives in our attempts at adulthood! The part we are unsure how to navigate is that which we never learned to copy.

I entered adulthood thinking it was much like childhood—just bigger closets and more freedom. There is an intensity to its responsibility that comes on slowly and yet all at once. "What do you want to be when you grow up?" would haunt me even a decade after I graduated with a college degree in psychology, as paychecks and prestige often define people's expectations for accomplishment.

My passion for serving patients and families, modeling for novice and experienced artists alike and for living a meager existence would have its unseen rewards. And in the middle of this discovery, I gave birth to my only child. You became both my student and my teacher as we navigated the necessities and pleasures of a life lived out on purpose.

She isn't a teacher by degree, although she surely teaches me
She has more compassion, than I can muster on my hardest days
She returns often with her affection and her praise,
what a blessing I received
In my...
My ever-present mirror, my child teacher, who I hold so dear
–Monica Rae

Chapter 5 – Is Faith Enough?

"I will have nothing to do with a God who cares only occasionally...We do not need the sheltering wings when things go smoothly. We are closest to God in the darkness, stumbling along blindly." Madeleine L' Engle

Dear daughter,

It was midnight; you were four years old, crawling beside me in bed, coughing and nauseous once again. This had been the landscape of many nights over the last two years as you waxed and waned through an unforgiving tether of sicknesses.

Months of respiratory infections led to surgery to remove your tonsils and anodes that left you hospitalized for over a week. This was followed by months of stomach intolerance and bi-weekly vomiting and diarrhea. As if these discomforts weren't enough, the parade of evil continued with a mass on your eye that grew until it was the size of a large marble. Three of these would occur in two years, all of which had to be surgically removed. The most obtrusive of these tumors took place during the autumn months when children were dressing up in costumes, and harvest decorations were sprinkled everywhere. On a quick trip to a local drug store, a clerk forgot to use her mental filter. She drew attention to the distinct tumor, leaving you to cry in front of a line of customers. This would be one of many ignorant comments of well-intentioned adults or unassuming children leaving me embarrassed on your behalf for months at a time as we waited for the next surgery to be scheduled.

But somehow that night I was prepared. For what, I didn't know. In the confusion and loneliness only parents of sick children comprehend, I was angry and without answers. I shook my fist at God. I did not doubt his power; I just questioned his love. Suffering begs the question—does God care enough to fix it? That night God would answer and bring the pain to a screeching halt.

"Now acquaint yourself with Him and be at peace." Job 22:21

I have filled your childhood with the knowledge that God loves you and that acts of service and fellowship can help define your faith journey. But these organized efforts to engage you in a faith-driven life are not meant to replace the intimacy that must occur between *you and your creator* if you want to know peace.

Faith is surrender, and that night I would become completely surrendered to the truth that God was more constant in his pursuit of me than I had been of him. His presence came forth like a patient all-encompassing power. I had prayed. Many had been praying for close to 2 years. Faithful, God-fearing people had laid hands on you in healing and anointed your head with oil.

And that hot, humid summer night as I lay beside you, I felt a presence so strong within me and around me that I spoke out in words that I did not understand. I learned later it is called 'speaking in the spirit' or 'speaking in tongues.' Regardless of the term used, on that night in my bed, I saw your illnesses being released from you. Within minutes your fever had subsided, your stomach symptoms were no more, and within months you would no longer encounter any stomach, respiratory or eye tumors. (Or so I thought.)

God brought me to that place of needing him more than I needed myself. I was awakened from my complacency and my human tendency to blame.

We make sure to maintain enough distance between ourselves and others, and even between ourselves and our own heart, to keep hidden the practical agnosticism we are living now that our inner life has been divorced from our outer life. Having thus appeased our heart, we nonetheless are forced to give up our spiritual journey because our heart will no longer come with us. It is bound up in the little indulgences we feed it to keep it at bay. – John Eldridge

History is heavily saturated with problems and challenges. Unlike bodybuilders who devote their attention to enhancing their apparent strength, God doesn't need to flex to show his abilities. His very existence permeates the world through all that has been created. Pain is universal whether it comes in the form of cancer diagnosis, job losses, broken hearts, bullying words, divorce or children dying in slum-cardboard boxes. It requires an overcoming presence, a power beyond religion. God shows us his power, not through his Santa Claus ability to check things off our lists of pain and pleasure. It is through loving us more than the pain we are haunted by! He knows what he's created and what we need. Our lives are the gift we give, to him, to others—lost in the intimacy—in a world full of pain and disappointment. This trust requires more than an emotional response on a Sunday morning or moral judgments toward anyone outside our comfortable ethical and cultural parameters.

I am filled with longing, as is the case for most of us, and yet my life is without a doubt tucked in the comforts of the Midwestern hospitality bubble. I see the paychecks rolling in, miracles of health and healing all around me, and I am grateful. That sense of gratitude infiltrates my perception of God—I have so much, how could I ask for more? Is it a feeling of entitlement or restlessness then, which causes me to look for the next project, purchase or person to satisfy my taste for a full life?

For all my religious education, Bibles stored and highlighted, church-going activities and serving the poor, it was you who would stir in me the greatest desire for spiritual clarity. After all, how could I ask you to follow if I didn't know why I believed? As a child, you became my sparkling mirror—reflecting onto me what I did and *didn't* want you to know.

Many women struggle to balance the demands of vocations, marriage, families and their interests. Magazine covers lure us into solutions to managing it all. TV shows confirm the myriad of emotions and expectations bound up with our roles. We look for justifications when work keeps us from a family night or desire to be at home with our children makes us seek out like minded mothers to fit in.

I can't speak on behalf of all mothers, and I see the need for all kinds of women in our societies. And yet, I know with certainty the day I learned of your conception my life was no longer my own. I was no longer defined by what I couldn't do, by the limitations of ongoing diagnoses; I had a clear purpose as your mother. I had been filled with a life completely dependent on me for months and looking to me for a lifetime. My concept of faith was and *is* challenged through my role as your mother.

So, it goes without saying that I would plead on your behalf to God. Making promises of faith that my all-too-clumsy nature would fail to keep. I exhausted all medical resources and home remedies to find a quick cure for your suffering and to ease my fears.

A seed of faith was planted that night that would take years of suffering to reveal itself. Through suffering, I would be asked time and time again if I had just enough faith to trust the peace I had been given.

The word "saved" in contemporary Christian terminology suggests we as humans are lost, wandering hopelessly in our lives and in need of rescuing. Who wouldn't rush to the front of the altar and receive this gift of love? When the spiritual high of a church service or abundance of blessings gives way to sleepless nights of continual prayer for God to remove our suffering, do I want him then? Or simply what he can do? Do I want peace—whatever I must endure?

Before I became a mother, much of my suffering came in the form of the demands of my ongoing diagnoses. And while I had attended funerals for neighbors and great grandparents, I had never known how the loss could be combined with clarity until I met Tristan, my dorm floor coordinator during my freshman year of college.

She was the first to greet me at my dorm when I moved to Sioux Falls, and I was instantly captivated by her aura of confidence and perfectly organized dorm room! It was her voice, though, that would haunt me for years.

During my sophomore year, she and her close friend asked me to live with them in an apartment on campus. I was enthusiastic and very intimidated. These ladies, only two years older than me, seemed more confident and self-assured than I was. I sought to be the perfect roommate by cooking suppers for us to share, leaving all the living spaces clean and welcoming. Unfortunately, one argument between the boyfriends Tristan and I had at the time was enough to drive a wedge between us for a few months.

So, I was pleasantly surprised when she came to me to ask if I would read over a rough draft of one of her term papers. Being a diligent scholar, I accepted the invitation as a peace offering. We had some laughs in the coming weeks and her smile was a welcome sight in the middle of the night when we took turns using the bathroom. When she had a cough and cold that seemed to linger for months instead of days, I encouraged her to seek further medical attention. She came home after the appointment led to further testing than would be necessary for a lingering cold. The confidence she portrayed reassured me that the testing was just protocol. Then she showed me the lump on her neck. As I reached to touch it, I was overcome with a sense of loss. And while I couldn't see the future, I felt a stirring darkness in my presence.

The day of her funeral, the church was standing room only, the balcony overflowed with those eager to get a glimpse. First the hymnals, then the contemporary songs filled the halls of the Baptist walls. But it was the recorded sound of her voice singing praise, the angelic voice of a woman now resting in the hands of her Savior that would move us all, even the children, to tears. Oh, how we wept. We cried in pain, the sadness that comes from saying goodbye. She was our daughter, sister, wife, friend, teacher and mostly our inspiration. To everyone she met and served she was the light—in her short life.

Over a decade later, I would come upon her picture in my college photo album. There we were, shoulder to shoulder in the living room of her parent's house and the silent whisper of her voice overcame my heart. The memory of her smile, the smell of candles in her room, the cheap pizza we used to purchase on Friday nights, the scarves she wrapped her head in when her hair fell out from chemotherapy, and the last days and weeks she spent enjoying her husband and her God. Our last correspondence was shortly before she passed away. We were going to 'catch-up' after she finished the rounds of her last attempt at recovery, an experimental treatment.

I would hear the whisper of her presence every June for years to come; humbled by the tremendous legacy she left in less than 25 years. It was her *confidence* in who she was that drove me to move outside my complacent lifestyle. I was 23, in the beginning stages of forming a non-profit and living on my own. I knew there was a God, and yet in so many ways, I was still lost. She seemed to know something that I hadn't yet figured out.

"Practice is the hardest part of learning and training is the essence of transformation." —Ann Voskamp

Two weeks after Christmas, when you were nine years old, your dad's truck had broken down, and he needed to buy a new one. Your grandmother was soon to have surgery 2,000 miles away, multiple friends of mine were sick or seeking prayer support for various reasons. Then, to top it off, my vehicle overheated and with repairs too expensive to fix we were now a home with one vehicle. Somehow though, all those heartfelt tugs and questions were quickly turned over, taking life in stride, choosing peace in the chaos.

During those couple weeks, you awoke one-morning complaining of sharp pain inside your eye. I looked closer and saw a chalazion tumor forming on your right eye. Unbeknownst to you, I had gone from faith to fear in a split second. I kept my face simple before you; I didn't want you to see my failings. I had let fear creep in. Maybe somehow, I hadn't prayed hard enough to keep the tumors from returning after 4 years without seeing one appear on your face.

As the day drew on, my conversation with God went something like this, "Really...is this a test? Am I being pushed to see how far I will trust? I don't want her to suffer, God." I became Peter at that moment once again. I reached out in my life for him, talked to him and responded to him, but as I walked, I fell. And in his mercy, I was renewed, again.

Would I only know full surrender to appreciation in poverty or pain? Maybe there is an element of surrender that must take place to live broken and full. Penetrating the mystery of faith seems daunting. Is that why so many walk away?

I can proclaim blessings and faithfulness to you each day, reminding you of the gift of life. But it is through my ongoing journey that I learn it is neither the absence of pain nor the abundance of faith that saves me. I had sought instant gratification through affirmation or affection from those whose opinions didn't matter, TV and chocolate binges when relationships failed, and used perfectionist tendencies to cover the lack of control that comes with chronic pain. Those approaches to life had failed.

We still walk hand and hand sometimes. You share your journal with me, how you were grateful for the day and prayed for the neighbor girl who hurt you with her words. I am rescued by your child-like faith as you teach me how to trust.

You were almost five years old, bouncing around the house in the same covering of joy you were born with. Remember the house on Holly Ave.? It was built in the 1950's, and the kitchen was an add-on. I was tucked in the corner of our kitchen by the counter-turned-into-desk area your dad had refurbished, trying to hide the emotions I was juggling. Papers spread in front of me as I attempted to balance the monthly budget, manage the diseases that haunted my body almost daily, and be content in a marriage that seemed to wax and wane like the weather.

You entered the room, your big brown eyes and two front teeth staring at me. You jumped up on my lap and hugged me, whispering softly, "It's OK mommy, It will be ok." Tears fell down my face. You knew nothing of the adult demands I was facing, yet somehow you saw straight into my soul, delivering a message of hope. As quickly as you jumped up, you jumped back down and ran off to find your kitty. I wanted to hold on a bit longer, your love a sanctuary.

"When you somehow pass your brokenness onto your own people, why does it hurt in a way physical pain never could?"
—Ann Voskamp

I am afraid you are like me. Tears quickly fall from your eyes, your heart so tender and sure. I am made stronger by caring for you and yet, your sensitivities scare me. I speak faith and yet I stumble— in front of you. Will you be impatient and anxious like me? Will you wander in a field of loneliness and physical pain? I don't want you to know my pain, but I can't keep you from experiencing your own.

There is no fair distribution of pain and peace. Along with death and taxes, there is the guarantee of suffering. Are we all not in the same place, asking the same question as Jesus did— "My God, My God, why have you forsaken me?" Are not our lives, then, journeys of surrender? He did not deny the existence of evil nor did he surround himself with only religious people. He was immersed in the messes of hurried and scared lives.

We hide behind our scars, sometimes ashamed or embarrassed. Attempting to cover up, we choose silence about our pasts and makeup for the morning. We ask, "How are you?" to coworkers, strangers and friends assuming all will respond "Great" with a smile to cover any pain. Why are we afraid of being wrecked or in need?

A scar is a tattoo that tells a story...

Jesus was authentic and unafraid of being broken. Fully vulnerable and fully alive and looking only to his father even in pain. Do I not have the same opportunity to live in full surrender, to trust even when I feel utterly alone?

The congregation sits quietly in thought and anticipation as the pianist plays "Nearer My God to Thee." My hands folded, trusting the symbolism of breaking the bread and drinking the wine that is about to take place. In this repeated ritual, there is faith and communion with one another and with God. I see the comfort of being reminded I am not alone, making my sad life filled with the beauty of love. I am no longer afraid of my wounds nor do I hide them as this book reveals to you.

"Mom, does this look OK?" You are wearing pink leggings, a long-sleeve shirt with a giant sparkly heart on it and socks in the shape of a kitty's face. I smile. You've never looked better, I say. You shuffle into my room as I begin to dress for the day and you, the dog and cat find your way into my closet. You search for the boldest color, a shirt in the shade of turquoise blue; you lay it on my bed and ask me to curl your hair. We are girls together as we play grown-up dress-up. I don't need to cover my pain today. The makeup and curls and sparkle shirts are for fun, for life-play.

Later, we double-check the tumor on your eye and apply the magic steroid-gel we pray will shrink the tumor *this time*. Knowing now, it won't be the last. I hold you close and see the questions in your eyes, the ones that you haven't asked yet. Someday when pain beats heavily on your door, I hope to be there to remind you what the mirror of you has taught me. In our brokenness…God's peace is always there.

Chapter 6 – In the Company of Men and Dogs

The essence of love is not what we think or do or provide for others, but how much we give of ourselves. Love concentrates so intently on another that you forget yourself at that moment. – Rick Warren

I met your father on a snowy day in January and it was, for me, love at first sight. He entered a friend's door wearing his motorcycle jacket and black steel boots. His face was beaten and red from the wind of a recent ride on his 76' Harley Davidson Shovelhead. He was tall, with dark hair and a grin that would make a woman of any age blush. The freedom he seemed to possess drew me in—I wanted to escape with him—where rules and responsibility didn't seem to exist. After only a few minutes of introduction and small talk, he excused himself to his downstairs quarters where he was currently living. Weeks passed until I saw him again. I thought of him often, imagining what I would say if I saw him again. I knew very little about him but my short time with him was enough for me to sense a great mystery and pain deep behind his eyes. I had never met a man who looked so strong and yet so fragile at the same time.

In May of that same year, I was due to have two surgeries two weeks apart. Having seen him again on occasion since our first meeting, I learned of his obvious love for riding motorcycles and often wondered what it would feel like to ride with him. He offered me a ride *sometime*, and I took him up on it before I was due to have my first surgery.

It was a Friday evening; the sun was going down and there was still a crispness to the prairie Spring air. He had me wear one of his faded red sweatshirts that were two sizes bigger than anything I owned. It was permeated with the smell of gumdrops and man sweat and probably could use washing, but I didn't mind. He advised me to wrap my hair up due to the damage the wind would do. At this point, I began to feel a bit apprehensive about my choice to ride a motorcycle with a man I barely knew.

The engine made a sound like nothing I had heard before. It sank deep into my soul, awakening something I wasn't sure I wanted to be revealed. He placed his hand on my thigh and spoke to me over the sound of the bike as we approached a red light. As I clung to him, I felt the world heightened around me in a wild and abandoned way. We spent a couple of hours riding through neighborhoods in Sioux Falls, and he reached back to reassure me with his touch. Maybe he knew I was nervous, but he never let on. As the sun passed beyond the horizon, we had escaped to a highway west of town. Bugs were stuck to my face and glasses; my hair was frizzed out in various directions, so I was thankful he couldn't see me as we rode a bit beyond the speed limit.

I had no idea where he was taking me, and I didn't need to…the *being with him* was my favorite part. We arrived at Wall Lake as he parked near the sandy shore and helped me off the bike. I burned the side of my boot and my leg on the side of his motorcycle. A portion of the melted black plastic remained on his exhaust pipe for years, and so did a scar on my left leg. Effortlessly, yet instinctively, he wrapped his arms around me as we listened to the water rise and fall against the sand.

To this day when I hear the sound of a Harley Davidson, I am taken back to the moment when I climbed behind your father in anticipation of the experience that at the time, I didn't know would change the rest of my life.

I laid in bed for a minute, staring out the window on the 2nd floor of the old farmhouse we were renting. Summer had officially drawn to a close in our corner of the prairie as noted by the slight chill in the morning air, which often occurred shortly after Labor Day. We had been inseparable since that first ride on his motorcycle, and now we lived together on a farm where the smell of fresh air and cow manure welcomed us home. As the wind blew in through the window, ruffling the cotton sheets, I was made speechless. He asked me to marry him. I was elated and quick to say yes, but for a moment shame wrapped around my heart. The guilt of 'playing house' was consuming my thoughts almost daily since we moved in together and I couldn't help but wonder if we knew each other well enough to make this life-altering commitment. I didn't relay any of my concerns to him, I just responded, "Yes!"

Your father is a man of few words but, on the rare occasion when he writes, his words explode with emotion and curl around my heart. But it was his touch that caused me to surrender, and to this day when he comes behind me and wraps his arms around me and holds on like he has no other place to be, my worries begin to fade and I am taken home in his arms. How would we survive loving each other this much?

He could rip my heart out and smash it. In the beginning, we didn't know we would do that to each other. The years would teach me how he could ruin me *and* restore me with a word...

In love we find out who we want to be,
in pain,
we find out who we are.

Photo albums are filled with the memories we make each Christmas, birthday, vacation and milestone. My mother had taught me well – for each picture had its place in an album that is carefully marked with a Sharpie pen by month and year. As I look through the pictorial memories of the many years with your father, I notice the eagerness that has overwhelmed me in my attempt to capture the perfect moments. Anyone turning the pages of my albums would take note of how time and devotion to family bled together to create the poses of our years. But somewhere along the way, I got tired of pleading for a smile to satisfy the yearly quota of picture taking or to create the perfect Christmas greeting card. I got tired of pretending I was happy in my marriage.

We had become roommates instead of lovers, co-parents instead of friends and my pleading for more intimacy, more closeness—a partner who looked forward to seeing me in the evening, who slept in bed with me, traveled, did life with me—seemed to fall on deaf ears. We were too different I concluded, we wanted different things out of life. I threw myself into mothering, my jobs, and serving. And each night after I tucked you in I would cling to my pillow and my bible, as tears ran down my face.

I must have made a mistake. I did not sense purpose in the marriage at all. Months turned into years as I felt disoriented and disconnected. I had to walk in blind faith, stumbling over myself, over my feelings of regret, confusion, and doubt.

It was early September as your father had returned from a work trip to Arizona. He had been offered a job at a clinic in southern Arizona, and I told him to take it. The long distance wouldn't be an issue for us as much of our lives seemed to be lived separately in recent years. For the sake of his children I knew he would turn it down.

For reasons that still escape me, he returned from that trip with a newfound urgency—to uncover thoughts and feelings I had buried deep in my mind for years. And with fervor uncharacteristic to the man I had known for over a decade, he spent every night that week peeling back the layers of doubt, fear and hurt I had bottled up for so long. He wanted to know if I was happy, if our marriage brought me any joy, if there was anything he could do to salvage and repair the wholeness of heart I had once placed in his hands.

I stood there in front of your father—makeup smeared my face, my clothes disheveled, words of pain clouding my perception of marriage. It was there at that moment when the memories of isolation, the pain of words you can't take back and years of habits that breed contempt were so intense inside my soul that I was broken. I had become vulnerable, laying it all before your father. And slowly I began to trust again.

So, for a few short months after a long ten years, I experienced what *I thought* marriage was and then just like a snapshot the moment was gone replaced with indifference.

Loneliness implies a solitude that beckons sympathy. So, how can it be that I have never felt more alone than in my marriage? And why should I stay in a marriage of convenience?

It would take me years of brokenness to begin to understand what could come from the ashes of hurt that lay scattered in the background of the perfection I tried to portray.

The 'D' Word

I was eight years old when I asked my mother about the 'D word'—divorce. At that time, it wasn't prevalent. One of my schoolmates was living with her mother and visiting her father on the weekends, and I wanted to understand why. My mom didn't have much of an explanation, only to say that some people did that when marriage was difficult.

At that age, I was just beginning to put together the image of marriage through the example of my parents. My mother tended to all things related to caring for our home and my sister and me once she got off work. My father chose instead to end his work week with large amounts of alcohol. His truck would skid leaving tire marks in the driveway and I knew he was there even though I was half asleep. He was verbally abusive to my mother, and if my sister or I were in the way, we would get a dose of it as well. After one episode too many, my mother gave my father an ultimatum—us or alcohol. Somewhere in the middle of my childhood, for close to 5-6 years, he gave up the beers but never let go of his verbal condemnation toward us. The suppers were never cooked right; the house wasn't cleaned at the right time; our use of time and space wasn't efficient in his eyes. I walked on eggshells all my childhood, hoping my attempts at perfection would gain his praise.

In high school, I heard my father making small talk with our neighbor across the street. Jan who was almost ten years younger than my parents had a youthful energy that surpassed even the children in her midst. The wall to my room wasn't thick enough to muffle the sound. *"Well, my first wife just left...no warning or even a note."* First wife? Wasn't my mom his only wife? It was shortly after overhearing their conversation when I saw him smoking and drinking again. Habits I thought he had given up that Saturday morning in 3rd grade when mom gave him the ultimatum. I realized then that he was someone I never really knew beyond his vocation as my father. Do I know life without the pain of his ridicule? In moving 2,000 miles away, did I forgive as well as forget or did I just cover it up with distractions?

My mother took refuge in her Catholic roots and the two daughters she had to raise. I am sure my mom pondered the idea of divorce when the drinking and verbal abuse didn't cease, but she never let on to my sister and I that it was an option. So, I grew up believing I would never marry a man that I couldn't stand up to. In many ways, I did just that, but was I ever important enough for him to get up off his couch for?

Divorce is a word your father knows a lot about. I won't attempt to share his journey with you. Ultimately your question to me will be "Why mom did you marry him if you didn't love him?" Sure, I fell in love (a few times actually). And when I fell in love with your father it was mutual, and it was effortless. But *falling in love*, my child, isn't marriage! And after the wedding photos are taken, and the wedding dress is put back into the box, and the honeymoon has long since passed, it's the marriage that is left.

I wrestled for years with the whisper to "stay." Maybe if I spend more time complaining about the type of husband I have or cry more tears about how lonely it is to sleep with my dog and cat while my husband chooses his couch and TV over me. Somehow, I reasoned, if I draw that picture bigger, maybe I'll be granted permission to get out, to start over. The answer never changed and when I began to stop shouting for what I didn't have, the sweetness of a creator's peace covered me in all the lonely places I thought would never get filled.

"The lure of the distant and difficult is deceptive. The great opportunity is where you are." – John Burroughs

Upon your father's return from his business trip to Arizona, there was a new look in his eyes, one I didn't quite recognize. It frightened me how much he seemed to care. I wasn't sure what he wanted or how long his attention would last. Over the years I had managed to put together the images of his childhood pain, the death of his father and various friends before meeting me, wives that couldn't manage to be married to someone who wanted to maintain the high school boyfriend status.

Your father never got to be a child in total surrender to his parents, wrapped securely in their arms and attention. They divorced when he was young yet maintained a close and civil relationship. Your father was left to be the man of the house in many ways, always on duty to protect and assist his mother and sister – a role he is devoted to even now, making trips to their homes to repair, clean up or provide whatever "muscle" he can. Consequently, in the freedom his childhood and teenage years provided, he became an adult the day he became a father at age 19, to your older stepsister. And so, he spent much of his adult life balancing the demands of an adult world of responsibility he wasn't prepared or equipped to take on.

Even after understanding what kick-started his habits, I couldn't seem to get over his lack of enthusiasm regarding our marriage. I had made it my mission to understand his 'baggage' to help him unload it. The heaviness of a burden he wouldn't let go of was suffocating me. I began to emotionally divorce myself from him. The loneliness seemed an easier burden when I stopped trying to convince him to care.

We all are a byproduct of our environment to some degree. Your father would seek out the hearts he could heal with his attention, just as he has spent much of his life making sure his mother and sister are well. His reluctance to judge or impose provides bruised hearts, such as mine, with a welcome place of solace and acceptance. I would fall into his net of dreams just as many before me had. He would cover me in a way I never experienced before. Where other men had been demanding and controlling, he was never in a hurry and was quick to laugh at my quirks. I was sure anger would arise when I ran his car into an ATM, burned his supper or didn't purchase the perfect gift for every occasion. More often than not, his response was simply his half-smile grin and an empathetic embrace. Your father has never asked me to be someone I am not comfortable being, even if that means he would rather be somewhere else!

Living my childhood in the presence of a father who had an alcoholic temperament, I became an overachiever. Every test needed to receive 100 percent, every paper I wrote needed to have the teacher's special smiley face or sticker. I lived for my father's approval and acceptance, even though I never knew that was what I was chasing. As a child, I unconsciously sought to avoid his wrath but didn't know life outside its shadow. As an adult, I see the circumstances surrounding the choices he made, the pressures of work, expectations of his generation and ultimately the alcoholic influence of his mother on his habits and temperament. I see a more complete picture now: from his soul broken in places he regrets to the newness found in being a grandfather. And his devotion to my mother's welfare has only increased in the almost 45 years they have traveled through life. I'm glad he is your grandfather. The echoes of what he has passed down to your aunt and me in our strong work ethic and love of animals is being passed down to you.

Your father's *'say la vi'* persona is both intoxicating and unnerving! He fell in love effortlessly and had no desire to set a date! It was okay that I liked managing the budget because he was better suited at finding sales on large purchases and settling up at the end of the year. A productive day for me usually involves chores and finishing projects left undone by time. Your father can pass the time strumming his guitar, watching shows on one of his four large screen TVs or browsing the aisle of Home Depot with no intention of starting a project that day...or month! When he is upset or saddened by unexpected changes he goes inward, sometimes for days or weeks at a time, leaving me to wonder 'where' he has gone and when he will return. When pressed too hard or in defending his insecurities he will lash out in anger and reveal his fears in ways that will later embarrass him. I was finally with a man who wasn't ready with a list of how I did something wrong, yet I had no guidebook on how to navigate such a dynamic!

Once a light was shined on the battle that was taking place in my mind regarding my disillusioned perception of marriage, I began to release my fears slowly. I had to begin to recognize that just as your father came with his own set of proficiencies and insecurities, so did I. Slowly, the layers of perfectionism are being gently pulled back. Instead of projecting onto your father what I wished he would be, I began to discover the peace I already possessed. I had always been accepted, wanted, forgiven and restored! I didn't need your father to save me.

Hurt feelings had flooded through the barriers I had built around my heart for so long. And yet, I now swim in the waters of clarity.

People marry for different reasons and they stay married for more than love. Chemistry, friendship, passion and pain they aren't confined to time or space. The years together have been sprinkled with separation, weekends of space to keep anger from becoming regret. I cannot give you the romantic movie version of marriage or even love. I can however relay the opportunity that comes when you let choices become teachers instead of regrets.

The years with your father have taught me to live one season at a time; rejoicing over the simple pleasures of watching you grow, gathering up baby ducks and kittens, meeting the winter sunrise with anticipation, soaking in a summer night's humid warmth, and watching your father's mustache turn white with the charms of age.

Marriage is scattered with the seasons of circumstances; when the sex drive inevitably changes and our ambitions and abilities become dependent on how fast our older bodies want to move, when our checkbooks get depleted from unexpected axle repairs because I would rather drive on dirt roads than the Interstate. I have become a student of your father's ability to breathe before responding. As you have seen me yell at the presidential debates on T.V., preach you a sermon before bed and lose my patience during math lessons you are aware, I am still learning!

In the beginning, the words "I love you" were used in abundance. We were like reckless teenagers, high on the lure of pleasure and hope. Unexpected cards and calls, making love and pillow talk, it seemed like it would never end. When it was replaced with seasons of indifference, I assumed your father no longer loved me. I saw marriage as a battle to keep his attention. As the years have passed, I no longer doubt his love, although I challenge his efforts. I despise complacency and have little interest in being his maid. And, he still loves, tests and disappoints me—all in the same day!

The struggle to be the best version of ourselves while bringing happiness to another is the paradox of any relationship. And the realization that you cannot demand that *only* one person was meant to fill your soul is the saving grace of ours. Love then becomes a choice (*one we don't always make*) but is given and received alongside honesty.

Both of us have exchanged our fears and dashed expectations for an opportunity to learn. My fear of being in a loveless marriage weakened me for years! This *perceived* loss had tainted my view of myself, of the person I could become! I had wanted certainty, but life wasn't like that. Was marriage a haven or a turbulent sea? How could it be both?

I sit staring out at the view that has come to own so much of my heart; the land sprinkled with evergreens and maple trees, birds breeding in wooden houses, ducks laughing in their pool and visiting farm cats appearing for chore time in hopes they will receive a reward for their assistance. The sun is fading behind the trees to the east and your father is sitting in his hammock listening to songs of rhythm and blues. He greets me with his smile. I am reminded of how humbling it is to be surrounded by such raw beauty.

"Innocence is the condition of deepest bliss" — Dean Koontz

If marriage fastened me into the complexity of adulthood than it was a chubby faced puppy that would beckon me to play.

When you were five years old, both of you were the same height, and by the time you were seven he weighed 30lbs more than you. He would go in your room to kiss you goodnight, find you when you were in tears and protect you as larger siblings do. And when you started a new dance class, sported a new outfit or were turning another year older—I said "Sit," and you both stood proud side by side for a picture. We met him when he was days old. Puppy ripples covered his face, big black eyes looked deep into my soul, and six weeks later we named our yellow Labrador retriever Harlee as he cried in the car all the way to his new home.

"This may be the primary purpose of dogs: to restore our sense of wonder and to help us maintain it…" — Dean Koontz

The baby itch had beckoned me when you were four years old. But more than another child I wanted a companion, someone to do daily life with. I struggled with my perceptions of marriage as your father went inward to deal with life's expectations. To solve all of these issues at once, I would throw myself into a new life—a puppy who would teach me more about living than people I had known for years.

While he was fully weaned from his mother when he arrived home with us, he would spend nights in his kennel crying out for the comfort she and his siblings had provided him. I tucked him in each night, covering his kennel with blankets as the books instructed; trying to elicit the feeling of warmth he had with his family. As though a warm blanket can be a substitute for a mother's heartbeat! But I followed the advice of the numerous books I had read and made sure he went potty before tucking him in. Only, the third night he was in his kennel I woke to a pitiful screechy cry, slightly different than the first two nights he had been with us. Of course, no one else in the house was awoken by the sound so in my motherly instincts I arose from bed, put on my sweatshirt to buffer the autumn chill I knew would greet me in the basement, and went to check on my dog baby.

I initially assumed I had been suckered into his call and would need to let his sad eyes cry it out. As I looked closer, I could see what the fuss was about. He had an accident on the other side of his kennel. I opened his door and picked him up, his kisses and fur a midnight hug.

I carried him up and down the stairs that went from our basement to the outside and showed him where to relieve himself in the damp grass. Nervously, he obliged and quickly returned to my side. He cried at the daunting sight of the stairs, so I picked him up and carried him inside. I gave him a bath and cleaned out his kennel. In all the commotion of the midnight hour, no one else in the house awoke. The quietness surrounded Harlee and me as he sat in the tub…both of us now wet and nervous and bonded somehow. Maybe he knew I needed him as much as he needed me.

Of course, the puppy years are like human toddler years on steroids as potty training was a 24-hour race to keep the house from smelling like a doggie daycare. I fastened a bell to the side door and set the timer for every 20 minutes and taught my dog baby to ring the bell with his nose each time he needed to go. Like an eager child, he enjoyed the challenge and praise, although on many accounts he forgot the order of things and would ring the bell after he had an accident. It's easy to look back and forget the pains of childbirth and remember only the bliss of new life. And while over eight years have passed and much of the demands of the puppy years are gone, we could never forget the chaos of those early years.

Like a teething toddler, he enjoyed trying new textures such as; heating pads, whole socks, loaves of bread, his bed, blankets, shoes, Polly pockets, whole bananas from the counter and whole cantaloupes from the garden. His favorite 'grab it when you aren't looking snack' is still tortillas (bag and all). He pulled out my tomato plants by the root and by six months old I had to replace the backyard wood chip landscaping with rock because he had consumed so much of it. He made himself known to the neighbors, running through yards, barking at strangers and licking babies…never aware of his size. To this day his shoe fetish has led us to create a separate entrance for shoe removal for all visitors, as one too many have left with half a pair!

I was assured by the vast internet resources that Labradors could consume more than smaller breeds without needing a trip to the vet. We learned to place things on the backs of counter tops and put all possible perceived dog toys away in rooms with doors closed. And I still checked his piles in the yard for the safe passage of all he consumed. But, one incident would leave me shaken and dialing the vet for advice.

Harlee was about a year old, and you, your stepbrother and I were going through childhood treasures on the kitchen table. There were erasers in the shape of cupcakes and footballs, cars that lit up when their wheels turned and at least two dozen pencils with sport team logos. We decided to go outside to play with chalk and water balloons in the yard. I instructed you both to put all the toys on the table away while I turned the water on outside.

You appeared moments later with matching smiles and swimsuits and towels in tow. The water fun was short lived, your brother appearing in tears after returning from a bathroom break. Harlee had retrieved the stack of pencils left on the table and scattered them all over the living room and kitchen floors, leaving only one untouched pencil on the table. With the water still running and you still in the yard I grabbed the phone and called the vet, certain we would have to make an afternoon trip to the vet to pump his stomach! The vet informed me that considering Harlee's size he would probably be able to pass the two dozen pencils in the coming hours and days. But that significant amount of pencil and graphite would have certainly been more damaging to a smaller breed.

After spending eight years updating a mid-century house in a small historic area of Sioux Falls, we moved to a small town just north of the city. Your father and I have always shared a love of the country, believing we would somehow end up on our own piece of land. With great anticipation, we moved onto our piece of the prairie with you, two cats and Harlee when you were turning eight years old.

Harlee is both curious and anxious, so we knew we'd need some fencing on our land to keep him from exploring the vast farmlands that now surrounded us. Luckily, the previous owners had left a portion of the property fenced. They had lined it with vines and a variety of flowers and vegetation that alerted us of each season by scent and bloom. One such anticipated beauty was the purple morning glories that climbed the height of the west-side fencing. Their beauty is misleading though. Unbeknownst to me, they are toxic to dogs.

After we had been in our new home for a couple of months, Harlee began to have daily bouts of vomit over the hardwood floors in the house. I assumed it was his adjustment to the new environment as he had been shedding like a sheep ready for shearing, a sure sign of anxiety the veterinarian explained to me. He also enjoyed grazing like a goat and trimming the edges of grass he felt were too tall, so I thought maybe he'd mowed down too much. But the vomiting became concerning as the weeks passed. I noticed him chomping away at the purple blooms. A call to the vet confirmed my fears. I brought him in, and he was put on a liquid diet and monitored at home for two days while I trimmed all the morning glories from his reach. The vet informed me a smaller dog might not have survived if they had consumed so many sweet flowers! Once again, my dog baby was saved by his sheer size!

Harlee lived out each day in anticipation and expectation of love and attention. As any dog owner will tell you, they have a personality all their own. And there are some habits that you can't train out of them. Harlee has always been determined to leave things cleaner than he found them. He licked the sink after we brushed our teeth, attempted to help with the dishes by using his tongue to wash each one I placed in the dishwasher. We noticed early on his love of kittens and made sure he always has a cat or two to clean and care for.

While work schedules and chores seem to keep me from making play a priority, he gently reminds me he is ready whenever I am! After a long day of work in the city nearby, I am welcomed home by the sound of cats' meows, a bunny jumping at his cage ready to hop and Harlee's tail wagging high in anticipation of our ritual greeting of affection. After I put my purse down and feed him his three scoops, which only takes him seconds to scarf down, we go together to tend to the ducks we keep outside. I turn on the water while he quickly finds his toys; I bend to retrieve his football and rubber froggie and rotate throwing them until his panting leaves us both in need of a pause. I sit in the grass, his eyes glossed over in pleasure as he licks the side of my ear. He's smiling; I know without even looking at him.

After the ducks enjoy their supper of kale, oats, and watermelon, they line up on the diving board I made for them out of scraps of wood and let out quacks of delight. We watch the ducks bobbing their heads in their fresh pool of water. The sun starts to move slightly behind the trees as we saunter inside together. I am smiling too.

Buddy, one of my many nicknames for Harlee, shares with me his excitement in mundane routines as he assumes his contented position under the table during supper, on the floor next to my side of the bed as I write, and outside beside me, as I dig in dirt or shovel snow. And while he never complains he doesn't have new clothes; he does presume I've bought him a new bone whenever I come home from Walmart. The demands of marriage and parenthood, of work and bills and laundry that never seem to go away are replaced with simplicity and wonder as I brush him on the back porch. This beast of fur has inspired me to be a child again—to understand the benefits of play that are only found in being fully present in the moment.

"We need another wiser and perhaps more mystical concept of animals. Incomplete, gifted with extensions of the senses we have lost or never attained, living by voices we shall never hear. They are not brethren; they are not underlings, they are other Nations, caught with ourselves in the net of life and time, fellow prisoners of the splendor and travail of earth." — Henry Beston

While we can't decipher all that animals and even plants have to say, we can observe them carefully and see the most amazing things. They are so happily instinctual and unburdened by the human tendencies of vanity and greed. Animals submit to natural selection; contributing to the circle of life that takes place here on earth. And while each species evolves along with their particular branch of life, they all serve a purpose. As humans, we have both the privilege and responsibility to observe and protect their well-being.

The therapeutic value of animals can be seen all around us, whether through observation, conservation or caring for our own. We pay to enter zoos to observe their habitats, go on safaris to be thrilled by their wild and untamed nature, we purchase puppies for our toddlers to grow up with and we laugh in unison at funny videos of our pets. They grab our attention as we regard their behaviors, not so unlike ours. And there are some, much like my Harlee, that are born with a desire to not only protect their human counterparts but who become our sermon on loving our neighbor through their ability to put our needs and reactions before their own.

As the years pass and I pause long enough to see it, I realize I am surrounded by two very similar teachers: man and dog. My husband and K9 extend unconditional loyalty and effortless affection, speaking more than their lack of conversation. Their all-inclusive living-in-the-moment and mastering of relaxation in the warmth of the sun calms my anxious tendencies and points me to a maker of my company and my bliss.

Chapter 7 – Prairie Sermon

Yes, this is how it was meant to be…where the traveler comes upon the gentle rose dawn awakening the birds' song and appetites… the awful glory of the sunset casting fire over the horizon…paralyzed by the beauty of Eden among us

Dear Child,

Three miles from our home in a town that was first called "New Hope," northwest of the busiest city in South Dakota, we drive the dirt road to the Lutheran Church on the hill. History on this hill is marked by fields of corn and hay and a small cemetery that keep the generations there over a hundred years later.

It's here where the stain glass windows sparkle in the sunset, children run around the headstones in their Sunday best and folks put on their best jeans to come and remember *who* provides. They come to hear the pastor's words and children's sermon and to take communion, but most of all they come to eat. Potlucks fill the monthly calendars sent out by elderly ladies who along with local farmers could teach a class on the history of the prairie. I would become a student and learn from them what it means to 'come home.'

"It will not always be summer: build barns." — Hesiod

People and experiences have been my teachers. Professors and assignments have driven me to search. Pain has revealed the greatest of lessons. But, the foundation of my faith was first built inside church walls and religious practices.

I was born and raised in an Irish Catholic family in the 1980's and 90's. My mother, dressed in her buttoned-up blouse with shoulder pads and dress pants, took us to church each Sunday, with my father getting dressed up with extra squirts of Old Spice, to attend holiday services and our milestones of baptism, communion and confirmation.

As a child, we are taught to 'be good,' and while this term contains different rules depending on culture and religion, the premise is the same; obedience to what is put forth by those in charge. No doubt, a level of respect for order and authority is healthy in every society. And now that I am a parent, I can appreciate the desire to instill morals and tradition into the life you lay awake at night worrying over. Yet, as a child I didn't understand the 'why' behind our church attendance or catechism classes with ambivalent teachers and restless children. I memorized the Lord's Prayer and could cite most of the 10 commandments, but I'm not sure whether it was the words of faith, spoken in between hymns I couldn't understand, or the routine itself that brought me comfort.

Looking back, it seems we were always preparing. The lace around the necklines of our paisley dresses freshly ironed so we looked the part on Sunday mornings. Laminated prayer cards memorized and kept inside baggy, shoulder length purses. At the end of every service my sister and I would follow closely behind my mother as she reached out her hand to 'Father' (the priest). My mother smiled as though she had been hugged by someone who knew her well and yet I felt my expected level of reverence was covered in an awkward confusion.

My faith practices shifted in my early teens when I began separately attending a Baptist church with a friend's family. Being invited to weekly AWANA activities and camps fed my pre-teen desires for being accepted. And while the Baptist church had trendier decorations, more memorizing of scripture and more bible studies then the Catholic halls I strolled through, I sense the many similarities in their attempts to keep people on the straight and narrow.

I was 17, in between boyfriends, full of hormones and curiosity and my mother had given me the choice between two summertime adventures, church camp or flying for the first time. I could join my Baptist church youth-group, riding the 4-hour bus ride, with the same kids I had spent the last three years with, and attend summer camp. Instead of looking at cell phones, we spent hours writing and passing notes, singing songs and playing I-Spy games with our like-minded peers. My other option was to travel by myself to South Dakota, visiting family that farmed land in the northern prairie and a week visiting a friend who had recently moved to the largest city in the southeast corner of the state—Sioux Falls. I chose the latter.

Over 24 years later, I wonder how different my life would be had I never boarded a plane for the first time traveling 2,000 miles to visit South Dakota. After my parents saw me off at the Sacramento Airport, I breezed through the security line which consisted of two uniformed individuals only slightly attentive to what was in the bags I traveled with—a stark contrast to the patience required for today's lines. Before taking off, I raised my hand to catch the stewardess' attention to inform her it was my first time flying. She was kind and carefully explained where I could find a map of the Denver airport so I could find my gate. I sat in the aisle seat for the first and only time after discovering the pitfalls of that location in relation to the food and drink carts. I moved here 14 months later, for different reasons than the ones that keep me here now but looking back I see how that first glimpse of a world outside my suburban routine ignited in me a taste for something else, something I didn't know I was missing.

Definition of theology:
the study of God and God's relation to the world

My mother's cousin was shuffling downstairs; I awoke suddenly realizing where I was—in a small attic bedroom of my second cousin on a farm in the middle of nowhere. I glanced at the alarm clock which said a bit past 10 am. The sheer curtains covering the room's tiny window let in the blinding light of a full sun cascading over a barren land. I dressed in jeans, a blue button up glittering tank and my new sandals—my obvious city attempt at country attire. My mother's cousin gave me a look of surprise as I wandered down the narrow stairs. She greeted me with 'good morning' as she busily prepared 'noon dinner' for her husband and others who had probably been up since the sun rose over the horizon. Her daughter and I were going to walk the land and then proceed to a local baseball game in the nearby town that was *only* a 25-minute drive away. The June landscape of a small town near Aberdeen, South Dakota was startling to me as we set off in the Oldsmobile at what seemed a snail's pace. I remember thinking 'there is nothing to do here' as even the baseball game seemed to be going in slow motion. Years later, I realize I was a suburban-raised teenager—ignorant and self-absorbed. Ironically, I now live surrounded by farms and dirt roads, relishing the vast landscape, preparing my hand on the steering wheel for the random car passing by. There is a slight tilt of my hand to the local whose car is covered with the same prairie dust.

As I was preparing to move to Sioux Falls to attend a Baptist liberal arts college, my faith consisted of rules I sought to follow. That's not to say there wasn't a relationship. I had immense respect for the God I'd spent years reading about. Bible stories echoed in my ears as I walked the walls of my dorm and classrooms. There were moral lines I was certain I would never cross in my attempt to get it right. I was so busy keeping him in the box I made for the god I thought he was, that I didn't really see him.

I typed up my long and heartfelt papers for the New Testament and Christian Living classes on the small Apple computer I borrowed from my boyfriend. Even then, when I thought I had it all figured out, I was searching. And as it happens when we are certain we have a firm grip; our hands begin to slip as our fears take control. It was then, after getting a degree in psychology and biblical studies that I began to wander outside the walls of the church. My moral tight rope had slipped, and I was reaching for anything that would keep me afloat. I had questions my professors couldn't answer, family who wanted me to return home and a curiosity that kept me moving. As is my tendency, I never do things halfway; assignments were tripled checked before being turned in! And so, I began to find comfort in the arms of men, who while not morally bankrupt, certainly didn't engage in meaningful lifestyle choices.

I spent years seeking solace in pleasing people in relationships. I seemed to be living a reflection of myself through the eyes of those who I would pour into. I didn't know who I was outside of the moral rules I thought should be followed. I longed for clarity—the comfort of my mother's Sunday chicken wrapped in the approval and affection from my father (that I never received). And so, when I failed and slept with someone I shouldn't have, when I didn't spend 10 minutes each morning in prayer or have my weekend evenings filled with entertainment, I was left lonely and anxious and afraid I was no longer loved.

Churches have the same mission: to know God and make him known. The difference lies in how this is executed. And since people are the builders of this community it goes without saying that there will be faults. In my years as a practicing Catholic, I felt immense guilt as I watched the seemingly flawless execution of the weekly readings, Eucharist and sermons. And yet, I learned to stand in awe of the beauty of these demonstrations of faith.

In the Baptist Church, the singing was louder, and we could follow hand gestures when instructed by the worship director. The youth rooms were filled with posters and activities and services weren't a carbon copy of the previous Sunday. But you couldn't dance in the aisles! A non-denominational church seemed to possess all that the other two were missing—loud music and dancing in the aisles, pastors who could get married and spoke with passion and personal experience (although often times, still long winded). But it was in this church that I was told you couldn't be baptized because your father and I weren't married.

An Assembly of God/Pentecostal church seemed to solve all my issues for a few years. I once again got wrapped up in religious routines; leading bible studies, nursery school teaching, outreach to newcomers, and insisting you attend weekly Sunday School classes where you brought back crafts and songs. It was in these same walls that I was often shunned for not having a husband who accompanied me to services and events. After a few years new leadership took over, I was given a rushed 10-minute meeting to explain how others were going to lead projects I had been heading. And while I loved singing with those leading worship, this changed into an audition-required position which along with the rest of service seemed to be about putting on a 'holy production.' The goal seemed to be about filling the pews not feeding the people, and so we left.

I wrestled in my understanding of who God could be outside of the church walls. Was I doing enough good if I wasn't fully engulfed in a church? What I found in the years of church and denominational hopping is a creator is bigger than his (or her) creation. And most certainly bigger than my attempt to define him. And peace is the *gift to me* when I am humble enough to receive it, whether I'm sitting in a pew or dirt pile!

So many of our contemporary churches operate on this same system of guilt. When our people are crying out for communion and rest, we ask them to teach another Sunday school class. When they falter under the load, we admonish them with Scriptures on serving others. One wonders what would happen if all activity motivated by this type of guilt were to cease for six months. Much of organized Christianity would collapse even as the Pharisees saw happen to their own religious system. As Jesus talked about thirst and rest, he brought people to the reality of their own heart...Nature bears witness. Picture an African lion, stalking through tall grass, closing in on its prey—the ruthless focus, the vigilant keenness...How about a mother brown bear when her cubs are threatened? Six hundred pounds of unrelenting fury. Now imagine you are watching one of these scenes not on the nature channel but from thirty feet away. Oh, yes, we find a very fierce intentionality in nature—reflecting the personality of the Artist. – John Eldgride*

Faith then is not found in religious tradition or Sunday school attendance. It isn't found in memorizing scripture or knowing all the apostles. These are *outpourings* of lives trying to live out their faith. These routines of culture and religion bring comfort to the wavering hearts of dependent humans. Faith then is seeing God. And during pain and suffering believing that *knowing* the peace I've been given is *enough*! His beauty is everywhere…

God sets out the entire creation—a science classroom—using birds
and beast to teach wisdom.

Even when you were in the womb, I knew you would have a determined spirit. Right away you told me (with your cries) what you wanted. I am as you are, very sure of my 'favorites' and so it is without effort that we engage in a mutual enthusiasm for animals. I was eager to fill your room and photo albums with animal friends just as my childhood had been scattered with them.

We had elected our first African American President, Barrack Obama after you turned 1 year old. An economic crisis had taken place throughout the country. Stock and bank prices plummeted, and the housing market's fluctuations were leaving thousands homeless and bankrupt. The election seemed to bring hope for change, transparency and community. People began to reach for change from the norms of the 1990's and early 2000's. Corruption and distrust characterized nightly news stories and so history repeated itself as people began to bring about change in their communities.

Home schooling, once thought of as the choice of families considered outcasts and religious zealots, was increasing in popularity. This time though it took on a different objective. It was the alternative to the public-school system's failings. A structure only 30-40 years ago completely trusted by families to prepare their children, now demanded from them endless hours of attention to fill in the gaps left by funding and program cuts. Merry Christmas was replaced with Happy Holidays, gym teachers were teaching physics because there was no one else qualified and schools trusted national appropriated test scores to measure the success of individual lives. In our great nation of freedom, we get to choose, and when you were 2 years old, I chose for us the journey of home schooling.

School was in session and there was a barking dog and a high-flying kitten in the classroom. You weren't disturbed by gossiping girls or bullies, I wasn't able to fill your classroom with siblings, but there would be distraction of another kind! It was common to hear the 85-pound K9 barking at the mailman right before history lesson, or your newest kitten attempting her morning wall jump with clawless paws before spelling. And the upstairs cat was always crying because at 80 years old she was tired of all the new additions to the classroom!

Your recesses would be spent with neighborhood dogs and cats, while longer afternoon 'fieldtrips' were spent chasing sheep, chatting with ducks at the pond and watching chickens pecking at the cat near by. Birthday invitations were sent to the cats at the local humane society and the wild rabbits that took up residence in our yard each spring were named each one by you—Brown Eye, Ruby and Buttercup. In your early years, we would save our bread and every 3 weeks walk a mile to the nearest pond to feed the duck and geese families that flocked there. Until we got ducks of our own and learned you weren't supposed to feed them bread!

One spring, we heard a rustle behind the garage corner. We went out together and looked up at the pocket where the roof meets the gutter and a house sparrow had built her nest there. She scolded us for walking by—trying to scare us off, fierce loyalty to the eggs she sat upon echoed through each screech. Through binoculars we could see her nest, lined with feathers, soft bits of bark, grass and wrappings she could find. When they were old enough, we'd watch the babies learn to fly. Each day they would fly further, one time a hatchling getting stuck in the wooden club house in the corner of our backyard. It was hard to tell whether the mother was screeching more for her baby to use it's set of wings to find a way out or for us to stay far enough away for her to not feel threatened. Eventually, he found his way and they both dashed back to the nest where the mother fed and cleaned her tiny runaway.

"And how shall we find the kingdom of heaven?" the disciples asked, "Follow the birds and the beasts," came the reply. "They will show you the way." St. Thomas, Apocryphal Gospels

Growing up I relished my animal friends. My parents would usher birds, fish, cats, and dogs and even at one point a cow into our family. A cocker spaniel mix named Sandy would accompany me on walks around the perimeter of our half acre lot. Buffy, a calico cat with a demanding purr would welcome me up the front steps of my parent's home and sit beside me on the porch as I painted my nails and waited for my friends to arrive. We would have parakeets that pecked each other to death, fish that had babies in our aquarium, kittens that brought home mice and peacocks that opened their wings and sang mating songs in our front yard. In my younger years, I was certain that my animals had the ability to communicate. I would talk to them endlessly, absolutely convinced that they understood everything I said to them.

It came as no surprise that after graduating from college I would sign a lease on an efficiency apartment that would allow pets—the first one a spring born kitten I couldn't wait to adopt. Samantha, a calico tiger mix, and an expert at sleeping would be my roommate through my 20's and 30's and your first spoken word (Kitty).

It was April and winter had overstayed its welcome, leaving ice and snow patches covering grass that was eager to change from brown to green. You were almost six years old and we were staying on a 10-acre paradise while our friends were away. Two of the animals in residence were pregnant upon our friend's departure and you and I would experience together the beauty and cycle of the animal kingdom. I woke to a screeching sound—like a mouse stuck between a trap unable to get free. Within minutes I would locate a year-old cat hidden between a workbench and riding lawn mower, sitting upon her babies. Her pregnancy had provided her with what her babies needed, but her young age instinctually caused her to play instead of parent. The first baby I would have to discard would cause you to cry and question my parenting skills as well! Unsure as to why I couldn't save this baby or why the mother wouldn't feed her young, you left a detailed picture beside their bed in hopes that the mother would be better informed in her duties. A couple more babies would die, and great sadness would overcome me as I wrapped them in cloth and threw them away while you were playing.

Another mother cat, Vera was also on the premises and would give birth as well. She nursed her babies as well as the other cat's litter. One of Vera's babies, the only one born a white ball of fur, bright blue eyes and clear Siamese markings, would become your first kitten. You would bring her home and name her Rosie Brooklyn and carry her like your own feline baby. She joined our growing collection of animals, cared for first by Harlee, our yellow lab, who insisted on cleaning her daily during her first year of life. Rose's piercing blue eyes never changed color and her stoic nature made her more of a furry statue then a lap warmer. And yet, you and I would mourn her when she died. When Rosie was 5 years old and sick with repeated and unrelenting stomach infections, I dug a hole in my garden and covered her with dirt and tears. As I approach mid-life, I find the need to discard the piles of the unused – the clutter of life and accumulation. And yet, I never tire of the addition of another animal to care for and I mourn the loss of each one.

Watching animals takes me outside myself, I become absorbed in their routines and unspoken emotions. And whenever I had to be elsewhere, I ached for them.

It's 15 below zero in January and wind speeds are close to 30 mph. I put on your bright pink snow pants because they are thicker than mine. Your father's large steel boots are perfect for slipping on as I make my way with 5 gallons of water, fresh alfalfa hay and containers of in season veggies and duck worms. This remains my morning routine through the months of winter and some may wonder why all the effort? For three mallard ducks who don't even lay eggs in those cold months!

I know why now. I go to church as I care for the land and animals. Their sermon of service, humility, gratitude and affection preaches to me as I start and end each day.

Church provides the people…the prairie provides the sermon

He was a 'one woman' animal. His devotion to me was absolute— my shadow, always behind or beside me. He was fond of the affection of many humans, greeting each one at the door, eager to lick their hands and smell their shoes, but in a 2nd best sort of way, his devotion and loyalty to me so complete spanning years. His name is Harlee, my yellow lab, now nearing his latter years. He has looked deep in my eyes, studied my voice and tone, trusted my hands and took it upon himself to be my guard. The birds, cats, ducks, bunnies and even dogs that require my time and efforts have taught me the profound beauty of service—an echo to the mission of church.

Every dawn the gentle sun rose in a crimson ball shedding a warm glow over the immense landscape. In the warmer months, the animals and plants seemed to wake up in grand anticipation of the heat. In winter, the sun's presence and illusion of heat would fall upon the snow like a blanket of fairy sparkles. The trees huddled together along the border of the farm to the north of our land. In the early morning the birds wake up the land with their songs of choice, darting between each tree and covering, whispering among themselves. A pair of blue birds come back each spring and dance for me. They serenade me with their song, if I am quiet enough to listen. I am mesmerized by the song of the prairie—the land and animals so instinctually moving together. I am made alive. And for the first time in my life I know I have come home.

A lovely land .... you can love it, but you can't control it. It's a
frightening thing.

The people of the northern plains are a brumating bunch, surrendered to the unrelenting winds of the prairie, captivated by the hard work and hospitality of its people. While we are less then 10 miles from the largest city in our state, we are separate in our affections for the land. Surrounded by farms and ranches we are influenced by their way of life and by their choice to raise another generation in this lifestyle of humility. Most of the farmers I've come to meet are diligent and humble. While technology has provided them with tractors, cell phones and weed killer they have been trained by their vocation to surrender to an unpredictable boss—the weather. And yet, they remain grateful.

Farming is a spiritual practice with willingness to descend into the grass. Out of the mess of the season, a crop lost due to infection, a corn stock that proved too short or tomatoes that never quite took off, there would be those moments when a few perfect veggies crept through the dirt. They'd rise above the rest, like trophies ready to be put on display. The reward of working the land comes not from a paycheck, nor praise of coworkers or even fans—but from the dirty hands, a sweaty forehead and stretched out shirt filled with veggies served for supper, given to neighbors or eaten right off the vine.

The life of the prairie farmer has taught me how to care for my ducks, grow my crops and trap unwanted pests. But it's more important lessons are found imprinted on my heart and habits. I see the beauty of my boots covered in dirt, the bunny tracks in the snow trail stretching to the land that guides me on the path less slippery and the smell of fresh blooms ushered into the house through the cleansing, whistling winds from the north.

"I pay tribute to God by paying attention" Ann Voskamp

Much like motherhood, marriage, teaching and serving I would find great solace in the ebb and flow, seasons and stress of working the land. My idea of "worship" has *changed* as I see the creator not confined to stain glass walls. His presence is revealed over the landscape of farms, rolling hills and tall grass blowing in the wind. He is fully present in the paradise of the prairie. In my Eden a creator meets me. He walks with me, whispering into my soul and I am made whole.

Where faith fills me, religion scares me

Sitting in a coffee shop after a long day of shuffling three children that I care for, I am certain I'd be asleep if I was home and yet I am awakened by the words of a local professor and theologian. His words echo years of historical and philosophical understanding and yet he challenges and shakes my tradition. But, I'm no longer afraid of what I don't know. I'm no longer afraid to question.

While there is much, I know for certain; that God created the universe and that evolving science and history influence our span of understanding and knowledge. I also know with certainty there is much I don't know. Not because I am lazy—although I've spent many hours binge-watching BBC drama series when I could be reading Calvin, Newton or Darwin. No, it's not only a matter of time management that leaves me unlearned or uncertain; it's the very nature of humanity. The very evolution of space, plants, animals and even humans consistently confirms we don't have it all figured out.

This in no way negates the learning, seeking or even questioning. Rather it is the absence of such that is concerning. How pious we've become when we feel like our religion or denomination has it all figured out—that enough imperfect people have come together to make a perfect rule book to follow. So then, where does a 140-year-old Lutheran church fit in? Will I be denounced if I admit I am not a Lutheran, that in fact I believe God is a more universal entity that religions all over the world reach for?

These Lutherans are a stark contrast to the raising hands of Pentecostals I once worshiped with. I'm challenged by this gathering of imperfect and humble people who chat endlessly about the weather and show up at your door with a casserole because they heard through the grapevine that you were having surgery. When the gathering room fills with friends and family for potluck and I watch you eat quickly so you can play more, I realize I am home for Sunday's chicken supper.

I could be accused of not picking a side—of being burned by the politics of religious institutions one too many times in my life! I am! And, I am ok with that. I am ok with being a home school mother of a child I had out of wedlock, who has a certificate to preach while maintaining secretary, nanny and modeling jobs because I would rather have enough to pay bills and savor over half dozen animals and land then be so busy working for the sake of accumulation.

My belief in an ever present and faithful God consumes my conscience and drives my desire for understanding and service to those around me.

When I moved to the prairie over 22 years ago people in California assumed, I was retreating to a barren land, void of beauty and culture. Midwesterners assumed I'd be returning to the 'sunshine paradise' after experiencing the ugly and dreary lull of winters below zero. I've come to find I no longer make excuses for either ignorance. The loyalty of the land humbles me and causes my heart to surrender to its beauty and power.

My faith is like the prairie, changing and yet the same. As I recognize all that I know and have yet to learn, I remain a student even as I hold status as a teacher.

Chapter 8 — The Extraordinary Lessons

"I cannot teach anybody anything. I can only make them think."

— Socrates

My daughter,

Long before the lessons of motherhood filled my horizon, the classroom of my life was scattered with countless 'teachers,' some unaware their words and wisdom would leave a lasting impression on my life.

The classroom was filled with glitter, ciaos and anticipation. She smelled of gummy worms and glue that had been gathering dust on the shelf of an antique store. At close to 70 years old she was far past retirement age for a second-grade teacher. But it was her confidence and eagerness that put many younger teachers to shame. Ms. Martindale would delight me for 9 months with her tales of Broadway, ballet and travels to countries whose names I couldn't yet pronounce. Her enthusiasm for knowledge of any kind would woo me into her classroom each morning and keep my attention throughout the hum drum routine of math, spelling and social studies.

This was 1987 and the public-school system in America was about to go through changes that would redefine how teachers would have to teach—the new goal would become a scoreboard of test scores the school, and ultimately the child, would be judged by. This change hadn't yet occurred in our district so many teachers, like Ms. Martindale, were still teaching from a style they had formed all their own, a simple passion for learning on display through the children's individual needs. Our class of 25 kids ages 7 and 8, sitting in groups of four gathered each day from 8 a.m. to 3 p.m. to play with a grandmother who taught us the huge gift we got to open when we learn. Ms. Martindale took us on field trips to see museums and watch the ballet. She brought speakers to our classroom each month that spoke to us about Native American history and real-life encounters with zoologists, scientists, and even a ballerina. Many of the speakers were surprises that she didn't relay to us until the day they arrived— grabbing our attention and making each week an unexpected adventure.

Our classroom, much like a family room, welcomed students and entertained quests. Ms. Martindale brought to life the lessons of our subjects, but it was also the grace with which she accepted each one of us that made us feel at home. Assignments were often altered to fit individual personalities as she was less concerned with uniformity or perfect test scores and more preoccupied with instilling in us a love for learning. She seemed unfazed by students like David who was so shy he froze in front of class unable to answer a simple mathematics equation. With no explanation beyond a smile and "Monica, I believe you and David will get along well," she paired him with me halfway through the school year. I thought she was confused in her old age, forgetful even, hadn't she noticed I was just as shy as David? How would we communicate with one another?

The wisdom of her years was astute in the weeks to follow as David and I created our own way to communicate through gestures, facial expressions, laughter and even quiet vocal responses.

Ms. Martindale never ridiculed David or me for being introverted, as though her years of experience had taught her what we had yet to learn—there was a place and purpose for the shy and melancholy. In the Spring, David and I would stand before our peers looking past them to our 'grandmother' in the back of the room, and read a short story we had written together, both filled with a quiet confidence that kept our heads up and sweating to a minimum. I would know David for the elementary school years that followed, but he never smiled again the way he did that year.

This would be one of the last years our school district would allow 'outside the classroom' experiences such as speakers, field trips and music programs—citing their expense and unnecessary usage as reasons for their cancellation. And while I was too young to understand the implications of such changes, I was old enough to be saddened when the bell rang on the last day of school that year. We would learn at the end of the school year Ms. Martindale had been forced to retire, our class had been her farewell party to teaching.

Early on in our home schooling adventure, when you were less than eager to tend to another math page or I was discouraged that my teaching methods in grammar were less than inspiring I would recall Ms. Martindale's legacy and the relaxed, living room setting she created that welcomed me into a world where knowledge itself was the gift. As your teacher I have aspired to a home school experience that mimics the wonder I found in my second-grade classroom so many years ago.

"We know what we are but not what we may be." Ophelia in Hamlet

"Why do you want to come *here* to study psychology?" the head of the psychology department asked me with an almost dubious tone. A naive eighteen years old having graduated from high school a semester early, I was considering moving 2,000 miles away from my parents and home in California to attend a Midwestern liberal arts school. His inquisitive manner was understandable. He was quick to highlight the harsh winters of the Midwest—maybe I didn't realize I would be trading the year-round glow of the sun for months of darkness and bitter cold. This would be the first of many responses from individuals who learned I moved from California. Great confusion overcoming them, a catalyst to "Why??"

After assuring him that a little snow didn't deter me from a great opportunity, we exchanged pleasantries and histories. Dr. Keith Jones stood a bit taller than me, dark eyes and black goatee and mustache. His passion for human behavior and the mind and how it inspired him to become a professor was instantly evident. He challenged my perceptions without judging what I had yet to learn. I shared a bit of my journey as a patient of a chronic disorder that led to more questions about the human mind, social expectations and the dynamics between the two. As we sat across from each other in a small undefined room for what seemed close to an hour, I instinctually knew that he was going to be a professor that I would never forget.

Months turned into years and Dr. Keith Jones became not only one of my favorite college professors, but my confidant and advisor. He would challenge my preconceived notions regarding criminal behavior and childhood development. When I couldn't attend classes on a regular basis due to constant sickness, he suggested I have a friend record the lectures, so I could replay them. He allowed me separate space for tests and agreed to meet me once a week to go over any questions I had regarding material.

During my junior year I needed to take Statistics 101 and 102. Dr. Jones informed me they were more intense courses involving more instruction that I could find difficult to keep up with if I couldn't attend the classes. I would spend hours studying in my small on-campus apartment determined to not fall behind even though shingles, immune dysfunction and constant infections determined my energy levels. So, when I agreed to meet him in the afternoon to go over my reports and tests for the course, his smile and words of praise carried more weight than the 'A' printed at the top of the page. He said I had done better than anyone else in his class and it was due to my diligence not attendance.

Dr. Jones would teach me more than I can remember through lecture and tests. Yet, his lasting impact is a constant reminder that knowledge doesn't end when class is excused and that my physical limitations could never keep me from achieving my goals.

For better or worse, step-parenting is self-conscious parenting.
You're damned if you do, and damned if you don't.

I became a student at 25, surrendered to the presence of a 19-year-old girl and 1 ½ year old boy, both children of your father. I would enter their lives in an instant and remain for a lifetime. I wasn't taking on the role of their mother as they each had one of those, instead I was called Jo Jo or Monica and referred to as their 'stepmom.' The awkwardness of this role would haunt me, bring me to tears and rip apart my preconceived notions of 'family.'

I had never been a child to divorced parents and knew nothing of how to execute this new role. Oh, I would throw myself mercilessly in for close to eight years, pouring out love into every detail of their two lives, before I discovered I had missed the 'step' part of my title. They had mothers, so they didn't need me to be theirs, but what could I give them?

It took a few more years for me to discover what my earlier years had prepared me for. During my childhood I had a 'stepmom,' not in the traditional sense as my parents were never divorced. Remember in the first letter to you I talked of our neighbors growing up—the Edwards. Through our journey together as neighbors, friends and ultimately family we would jokingly refer to them as my 'stepparents.'

She didn't have to 'mother me' to be my other mother

Jan had given me the example I needed to perform my lifelong role as a stepmom. I no longer needed to 'try so hard,' expecting it to be the mother/child relationship you and I will always cherish—it would be different. And with that realization came the skill necessary to love them, just as she had loved me. Jan would give of herself. She would literally share her journey with me, her passions and her prayers. And together we would share a love of art and animals and once I got older a shared appetite for wine. Lots and lots of wine!

Miles separate us now; my stepmother turned to friend over the years, the warmth of her embrace enough to take away worries, the sound of her passionate voice lifting my spirit to a place of renewal. And yet, it began with the mundane and routine as she picked me up from school and brought me smoothies in the summer when I was in pain. Her cartons of homemade fudge arrived a few weeks prior to Christmas each year which were just excuses to gossip about boys and life. But it was the example she lived out that spoke the loudest.

Her home and the land that surrounds it is an artist's canvas. Every square inch serves a purpose in color, pattern or inspiration. Sculptures she's designed lay against greenery native to the valley heat. Floors, tables and counters are meticulously clean and every towel, wine glass and book have a precise location. While these tendencies border on OCD, I can relate to the contentment I find in order and purpose in my own home. While I would curl up in blankets and books at my parent's home, I would saunter across the street to meditate in the museum of inspiration she created. The colorful life she lives on purpose inspires every role I take on. And I could finally begin to execute my role as a stepmother—knowing full I had been given an example of love in her.

Always know where you are

She stood in front of her quaint corner house, her light brown hair pulled back and small black dog in tow. She carefully examined me, unsure of what to make of my relationship with her father. I learned quickly that she held the same protective glass wall in front of her heart—much like her father—trust built over time, but kindness offered without reservation. Her hesitations were understandable for I was 14 years younger than her dad and only 6 years older than she was. For months I would attempt to 'woo' her, offering her the assurance of my affections and intent toward her father. One evening three months after we met, I stood in the parking lot of Gordman's clothing store and spoke the words I would remember years later, "I love your father, but more than that I like him."

Every couple years, you and I make a trip to California to visit my family. On one of these trips your father and stepbrother joined us. As is the tradition in my family dozens of photographs were taken by my mother with multiple copies printed and shared in the weeks following the trip. The day before we were to board the plane and return to the prairie my sister had plans for us to have our pictures professionally taken at the nearby JCPenney's studio. With coupons in hand and sunburned faces from a recent trip to the beach we entered the studio taking various organized photographic shots of our time together. I smiled as I had done so many years before to provide my mother with the comfort these photographs bring her in my absence. And I shared these images with others, including your stepsister upon our return home.

As I hadn't signed up for 'step-parenting 101' in college, I was ill-prepared for her response to these studio-taken photographs. She informed me that I shouldn't have allowed a picture to be taken with her father, myself and his other two children without her being present. That it wasn't a fair representation of his family. My defenses rose quickly, for while I was in no way trying to insinuate, she wasn't a part of the family, I agreed to the studio pictures for my mother and sister.

After much discussion and a few years of failed attempts at connection we found a lasting bridge in the form of a baby. Your father and I have become 'Papa and Nana' to two beautiful girls of your stepsister and her husband. The grand girls climb on our laps as your father's children and your sister's husband fill in around us. Family pictures now are taken on a faded wooden bench covered in bird seed on our land.

When I first met her, this adult-child was searching for the comfort and assurance that comes from union. I couldn't undo what her parents and other figures in her life had already impressed upon her life. As much as I wanted to replace her memories with the assurance that marriage and family can be a healthy and loyal refuge, I could only show her the beauty that can come out of the ashes of our lives. Much like your father, your stepsister is full of dreams. They love at a distance for fear of revealing too much and yet they remain loyal to their family and friends without judgement. While I may have failed her early on in my attempts at a role neither one of us could truly define, we have formed a family now, a legacy for her children to find refuge in. Her free spirit inspires all who know her, to dream.

There's this boy who stole my heart, he calls me Jo Jo

He came with your father over to my apartment on a Sunday afternoon for Chinese takeout. He was toddling around, chasing my cat, ripping pages out of my cookbooks but not saying a word as his pacifier was securely tucked in his mouth. Your stepbrother was 1 ½ years old and easy to love.

Shortly before he turned two, we moved into a farmhouse outside of Sioux Falls. It was in this house that we formed a family routine. Each Saturday morning, we had him, I would rush downstairs to the tiny kitchen and start the scrambled eggs. He would tug at my pajama pants and gesture to be held so I would hold him with one hand while I stirred the eggs we'd serve to his father.

Within months he began to refer to me as Jo Jo, whether from a TV show or his own creation it stuck and to this day I relish the sound of my name when he calls me. It is so easy to fall in love with a child and I would fall for this smaller version of your father. Together we would play ball outside and inside, we'd rock in the hammock and bake cakes on stepping stools. And at daycare drop off he'd inform his little friends that I was his Jo Jo, as though they too must have one. We watched him grow, I cried when he entered kindergarten and worked in his classes for part of his elementary school years.

While I was busy trying to be his mom, I would lose sight of the one he already had. I couldn't keep up with the love affair they shared with sports so as the double digits approached, I was forced to step back in my role in his life. This was a painful experience, going from seeing him every week to going weeks without seeing him. For years I froze in his company, too overwhelmed with bitterness and embarrassment. How could I let myself care that much?

I spent years seeking to woo him back to playing ball with me against the wall again. He became a teenager, began to drive and was wandering. The allure of the freedom of age had won. I became a figure head, the stepmom who lures him now with the promise of his favorite meal or ice cream cake. Maybe someday he will return, with a woman or child or the realization that we are *cooler* than the way his 'teenage glasses' portray us.

The word 'step' implies separate, addition, not a part. I despise this connotation. Every time I hear from your siblings my heart skips a beat; do they know I'm just the same? 'Step' is a part of my title too. We are both parts of a whole. Love is once again the teacher, the choice and the challenge.

"It is truth that climbs off the pages of Scripture and leaps alive into your arms when theoretical beliefs in a Creator give way to experiencing the act of creation." Lisa Jo Baker

It's true a mother's love is biased and never ending. It's a love that forgives, accepts, excuses and justifies. In its greatest moments it's pure and inspiring like a young fawn learning to stand after birth, its mother gentle and believing knowing her young through scent and touch. And yet a mother's love remains instinctual—seeking protection at all costs like a hovering hawk never far from her young—ready to devour any predator that gets too close to her young.

I would know this love the moment the midwife handed you to me and I breathed a sigh of relief you were well and still near. From that moment on my soul was altered as I surrendered to all that motherhood would teach me.

We arrived at the hospital in late afternoon on a Wednesday. I was 37 weeks and 6 days and had been to my weekly appointment. Everything continued to look as it should, you were measuring well, and I was dilated to 2 centimeters. But another glance by my midwife, Lisa, revealed that I was defacing, which meant that I could potentially go into labor at any moment.

Lisa was stoic and raw and her passion for babies and the women who carried them spilled out into the hours she spent with each patient. I trusted her completely, I needed to, she would be my guide through months of late-night phone calls, Braxton hick's contractions and the process of labor—something no woman can be truly prepared for.

She moved things along by releasing my membrane and within an hour I was contracting, and your father was on his way to the medical office. We made a quick trip home to pick up my bag that had been packed for months prior and I hugged my cat Samantha goodbye assuring her I would return with the life she had been keeping warm in my belly each night. We checked into a birthing suite and began the check list of my birthing plan! Like most plans though, mine was about to change as the contractions came on quicker than anticipated, the warmth of a hot shower wasn't easing them, and I seemed to have less and less control over the pain.

My midwife was fully aware of the demands of my illnesses on labor. And while you and I were never at risk, she was concerned that my pain and fatigue levels would become too intense for my body to facilitate pushing so she suggested that my water be broken manually. Labor was intensifying as I felt myself disappearing under the heavy sea of pain I wasn't mentally prepared for. I was certain I couldn't do it until the epidermal took affect! As I moaned with each contraction, I saw your father's face. A wave of relief seemed to overtake him as I gathered my strength and began to push. Within a few hours I was looking at a mirror at the top of your head covered in dark hair being pushed out from me. As the story has been relayed to you on each of your birthdays your cry was heard from the hallway as nurses peaked in to see the new 'pink' arrival that had the lungs of an opera singer.

The air was crisp on a Saturday on the last full weekend in May as we left the hospital with our new baby in tow. I was certain I was prepared for what lay ahead of me. It was like a superpower had come upon me. My breasts fully engorged—your food source for the next 13 months, my diaper bag filled with books from the midwife, instructions from the nurses and my already-detailed calendar awaiting me next to your changing table where I would record every feeding and diaper discharge for the first month.

I was on call 24 hours a day, in full surrender to your cries for hunger, warmth and play. Motherhood was alluring in all its newness yet misleading in all its unknowns.

The truth is there is no road map, no matter how good your example was or how many books you've read. It's learning to ride a different kind of bike and the only way to do this is by falling over and over again. I was becoming someone else. Stretch marks, wrinkles and changing breast size, free time that no longer belonged to me, endless conversations about diapers and each new thing you said and did...my life was no longer my own.

When you were colicky as a baby, I would rock you in front of the Cosby Show from 5pm to 9pm each night—after a few weeks of it I thought I was going crazy, hearing your cry echo my ear drums long after you had fallen asleep. The nights I would lay up with you when fevers, vomiting and eye discomfort would overwhelm you would leave me exhausted and at a loss in my attempts to take it all from your innocent body. The terrible 2's and 3's were marked with tantrums that had me slamming doors more often than you. By the time you were 8 years old the toilet training and tantrums had long since passed, replaced with the clashing of your independent spirit and your fear of the unknown. When you hit the double digits, I saw you as you have always been, just taller and able to form more sentences. Still you were a giant heart walking around full of compassion for every bird fallen and every person's tears.

"We see in ourselves our children better than in any mirror"
— Lisa Jo Baker

I grew up, I had to, my legacy would be reflected in your eyes and ears. A sense of urgency seemed to overcome me as I wrestled with the reality that you would come to know me not just as your food source but as your provider, your confidant when you were sick or sad, your teacher and in time I prayed your friend.

Children disguise nothing. As mothers we are pulled into the naked truth of our children—the diarrhea on the brand-new sofa, the tantrum in the airport because I left your favorite pink blanket on the plane, the throwing of rocks at kids at the playground, or the complaining in front of my co-workers about how many chores you have. Yet, as the years pass quicker than the days, the awkwardness gives way to a new name as *Mother*, which seems to fit nicely—much like my 10-year-old pair of grey yoga pants, the ones with the holes in awkward places and elastic about to give way.

Every mother has her own struggles whether it's an absent husband, an overbearing mother in law, a disabled child, or a demanding career outside the home and it all has a defining effect on her role as woman and mother. We become vulnerable, unsure of how the role will change us...not certain we want to change. Our hearts become bruised, torn, filled, opened and ultimately renewed with the presence of a life so utterly dependent on our influence.

The other mothers understood this—everything I never had to express in words—they heard and mimic with their sighs of understanding. As though we knew we were in the trenches together. We would support each other through emails, texts, prayers and the rare moments of uninterrupted conversation. And then we'd return to the never-ending piles of laundry, bills that are ready to be mailed only to find the check never made it inside the envelope, meals that don't get eaten because most of it was thrown to the floor, navigating tantrums and toilet training like someone had enrolled you as a sergeant in boot camp, and requests for water and one more hug when it's 30 minutes past the first time you tucked them into bed.

The romance of motherhood that spans cultures

She sat beside her only possessions—two suitcases filled with clothes, shoes and any trinkets she could fit inside. Curled up asleep in her arms was her 3-year-old son. They had traveled over 20 hours, tagged at multiple airports, refugee/immigrants from a camp in Malta. Tseigeweyni was born in Eritrea, Africa and she fled her country's poverty and persecution in pursuit of a better life. After seven years as a refugee she sought the freedom of America. Using gestures and broken English to communicate we began to form our friendship at midnight in the airport. It started as a sponsorship, an opportunity to work with the church and social services to assist a new immigrant arrival. Days turned into months and mother and son crawled into our hearts.

"Monica, you learn me lasagna?" Tseigeweyni asked as she opened her oven door. I smiled and said, "Of course." We sauntered through the local grocery as I explained the term 'sale' and we take turns guiding her son through the aisles, finding the ingredients needed for our lasagna. We spend the day together doing tasks that I rarely find myself fully present for. I order my groceries online each week, without the energy for strolling through the aisles. And most meals I prepare alone, quickly, while tending to unkept chores of laundry, cleaning and bills. But here in her tiny apartment we cook together, we laugh, we talk, and you join us as we sit together and eat it right from the oven. She teaches me the art of tea making with special seeds she soaks in the water in her kettle. And we sit and talk about our lives, the men, the love of our child and our families that are miles from us.

The most sacred of opportunities…
to see the world through someone else' eyes

"Mom, this is a good change," you said, as we drove from Tseigeweyni's apartment to our acreage northwest of the city. Some weeks we spent multiple days or evenings with them, taking her to English classes, showing her how to navigate Walmart and Hy-Vee grocery stores, introducing Francesco to the thrill of parks, animals and new friends and endless teaching of English words and American culture. I could see in your eyes what I felt in my heart—in the giving, the sharing, the laughing—we were free and filled. We became students together, learning from Tseigeweyni and Francesco, the heart of their culture and language. In the luxuries of our American lifestyle, we will never know the memories of poverty and fear she spent nights crying over. We will never understand the strength she has clung to in order to leave her family and home for a better life.

We bring them books, food, toys, a TV and she serves us chicken and homemade bread and bottled water. And you may remember the fancy white sandals from one of the suitcases she came with. She placed them in your hands as we left one afternoon, and you hugged her. You wear them differently than the ones you got from Old Navy. Her sweat, her story, her heart is now a part of us.

A year later, she has moved to another city, hopefully less afraid than she was when she first arrived on American soil. I was reminded of her native culture as you and I spent a Saturday morning with a neighborhood of people in downtown Sioux Falls. We join for a lunch, we play with their kids and a local minister Rebel, brings a word of hope with a team of encouragement. William, a tall beautiful man, his skin the color of chocolate, his spirit one of peace asks to sing "Amazing Grace" in his native tongue, Dinka. I stood in the front, gathered a little one in my arms and swayed to the sound of his truth. I looked at you, standing beside me, wondering if you felt the beauty of his pain through the words.

In my pursuit of the perfect legacy I leave you instead a patchwork of imperfection and grace, inability and service, misperception and passion.

It's early autumn, I'm preparing for a wedding ceremony I've been asked to perform. I have known the soon to be husband for as long as I've known your father. He's found love again, later in life, and he and his bride want to solidify their feelings with commitment.

They've asked me to guide them in writing their vows, words they will say in front of family and friends, declaring their choice. I'm humbled to bring them a moment—a celebration of the vulnerability of their hearts. And I'm reminded to surrender, to trust in the peace that comes from renewal and to share with others the opportunity to do the same.

Every person has a story, a unique mix of the routine and extraordinary. And lives become intertwined in the details, the places we can relate and connect to. The journey is a blessing and a challenge and with that lessons are taught and learned.

As a mother I would like to protect you from bullies and heart breakers. I ache when you cry and my heart sinks to my stomach each time you learn more about the darkness that exists in this world. As your mom, I will have forgotten things, disappointed you and left you with more questions than answers, but ultimately, *I trust more in your abilities than in my flaws.*

I know you will come to learn as I have. The extraordinary lessons in this life are found in the middle of pain's chaos, when hope is a stranger and relief is but a dream and you are able to surrender to a place outside of yourself. A place where loss becomes an opportunity, fear compels you to push beyond your abilities and the 'teachers' you surround yourself with expand your ability to love.

While this is the last of the letters, I write to you, I have no doubt that you will teach me more as we journey together. I will do great things in this life, the most exceptional found in the reflection of being your mother.

"It is not the critic who counts, not the man who points out how the strong man stumbled or where the doer of deeds could have done better. The credit belongs to the man who is actually in the arena ... who strives valiantly, who errs and comes short again and again, who knows the great enthusiasm, the great devotions and spends himself in a worthy cause, who at the best knows in the end the triumph of high achievement and who at worst, if he fails, at least fails while daring greatly, so that his place shall never be with those cold and timid souls who knew neither victory nor defeat."

— Theodore Roosevelt

The Middle of Ordinary: **Lesson Guide**

Use these questions to guide your reading, reflect on your own journey or to share in a group format!

Chapter 1 – Pain's Purpose
"The greatest teacher you will know will be the journey just past your comfort, the place where fear and torment tease your spirit, and you wonder if you'll ever find relief."

1. What 'pain' takes you past your comfort zone?
2. What 'fears' torment your spirit?

"It's there that you will begin to understand what you are capable of. It will scare you, my child, and make you wonder where God is, and when you realize you are being carried, it will finally become clear how strong you are."

1. Has pain ever been a teacher for you? Could it be?
2. When have you questioned God's presence? When or how have you been reassured of His power?

Chapter 2 – The Point is to Serve
"I do not know what your destiny will be, but of one thing I am certain—the only ones among you who will be truly happy are those who have sought and found how to serve." Dr. Albert Schweitzer

1. What does this quote mean to you? Personalize it. Define 'serving' in your life?
2. Do you think this quote is true? Why or why not?

"A word came to me in secret, a mere whisper of a word, but I heard it. I had no choice except to surrender to it—the voice was one of peace and clarity of purpose…"

1. When have you had clarity of purpose?
2. What are you struggling to find peace in currently?

Chapter 3 – Cul-de-Sac Roots

"I suggest that you revisit what shaped you—the innocence of childhood, the roots and routines that sprinkled your early years. Don't seek to mimic your past for the sake of tradition, though. Instead, gain discernment, laugh and rejoice at milestones. It will be a timeless teacher."

1. What are some of the fondest memories you have of your childhood?
2. What legacies are you thankful for?
3. What 'roots' or childhood relationships have left a scar that you are still processing?
4. What are you grateful that you learned from your parents that you want to share with others?
5. What will you do differently?

Chapter 4 – After Innocence

"I entered adulthood thinking it was much like childhood—just bigger closets and more freedom. There is an intensity to its responsibility that comes on slowly and yet all at once. "What do you want to be when you grow up?" would haunt me even a decade after I graduated with a college degree in psychology, as paychecks and prestige often define people's expectations for accomplishment."

1. What has surprised you about adulthood—in your 20's, 30's, 40's and beyond?
2. What did you want to be when you grew up? Why? Did it change?
3. How do you value accomplishment?
4. What expectations or pressures did you feel or do you feel now that influence your choices? Another words, what is your 'adult peer pressure?'
5. If you are 40 or older, what have you learned about other people's expectations and how you let them affect your life?

Chapter 5 – Is Faith Enough?

"Unbeknownst to you, I had gone from faith to fear in a split second. I kept my face simple before you; I didn't want you to see my failings. I had let fear creep in."

1. What are you afraid of?
2. Is it God you want or his ability to give you what you want?

"But it is through my ongoing journey that I learn it is neither the absence of pain nor the abundance of faith that saves me."

1. When do you feel strongest in your faith?
2. What pain is currently crowding your peace?

Chapter 6 – In the Company of Men and Dogs

"The lure of the distant and difficult is deceptive. The great opportunity is where you are." – John Burroughs

1. What distant opportunity or achievement are you certain would make your life 'better'?
2. What current situation do you want to escape from or be released from? Can you learn anything in the presence of the difficulty you're facing?

"The essence of love is not what we think or do or provide for others, but how much we give of ourselves. Love concentrates so intently on another that you forget yourself at that moment." -- Rick Warren

1. It's easy to love when we are loved in return. Who inspires you to love and not be concerned with what you receive? (person or animal)
2. Who is it a challenge to love? What do you learn from that person?

Chapter 7 – Prairie Sermons

"The loyalty of the land humbles me and causes my heart to surrender to its beauty and power. My faith is like the prairie, changing and yet the same."

1. How has your faith, your journey with God shifted, changed, evolved in the last 5 to 10 years?
2. Do you struggle with religious expectations and a relationship that feels like your own?

Chapter 8 – The Extraordinary Lessons

"The most sacred of opportunities…to see the world through someone else's eyes"

1. List 3 people that have taught you a different way to see a situation or the world around you?
2. List 3 people you have been given the opportunity to teach, help or pour into? How are these 'students' teaching you?

"The extraordinary lessons in this life are found in the middle of pain's chaos, when hope is a stranger and relief is but a dream and you are able to surrender to a place outside of yourself. A place where loss becomes an opportunity, fear compels you to push beyond your abilities and the 'teachers' you surround yourself with expand your ability to love."

1. When has loss become an opportunity for you?
2. When has chaos humbled you?
3. When has fear compelled you to move beyond what you thought was possible?
4. What has this book helped you to consider?

ACKNOWLEDGEMENTS

One Autumn evening, I was sitting in the living room debating the most recent news stories. I had gone off on some tangent, expounding on my opinions. With his eyes on the TV, my husband relayed, "*You should write a book.*" Thinking he was being facetious; I dismissed his suggestion. But then, I started thinking…what if?

Thank you to Larry and Cathleen for editing my manuscript. Your suggestions guided my writing, your encouragement and support drove me to dig deeper. Thank you to Steve, Barb, Lara and Mom for being my 'readers,' so responsive with each new chapter. Thank you to Emily who did the cover and cards. Your skill and smile are like sunshine.

To Mom, your unfailing support and love is the reason my Emma bares your name. To Ursula and Mike, Mom and Dad and the Edwards who have always kept the door open to my first home!

To my 'teachers': Dawn, Britt, Lara, Annie, Arden, Benton friends, Artist friends, Savannah, Charlie, Henry, Caroline, neighbors, family and friends near and far!

To Hun, your acceptance is fueling and I'm better for it!

To my Emma, you've heard my words your whole life, now the details are in these pages just in case you forget! *And thank you for spending a Sunday afternoon taking pictures of your Mama for this book!*

ABOUT THE AUTHOR

Monica lives on an acreage outside the thriving city of Sioux Falls, South Dakota. Diagnosed at a young age with a chronic immune disorder she took refuge in helping others. After running a non-profit for 8 years she turned her focus on mothering and home schooling her daughter. She works as an office assistant, nanny and model—having spent close to 20 years modeling for various artists in Sioux Falls. She relishes her weekends when she can be found filling her ducks' pool and lounging with her dogs while reading her stack of weekly finds from the library.

Thanks for reading!

Stay in touch! I enjoy hearing from readers and love sharing with groups of any size! Request a speaking engagement for your group or gathering. Or stay in contact to receive information on my NEXT book! Thanks again!

Monica Rae

middleofordinary@gmail.com

Monica Rae

49543763R00097

Made in the USA
Lexington, KY
22 August 2019